KT-564-113

CHAPTER ONE: DOMESTIC VIOLENCE

Abuse in the family

What's happening at home? We all have the right to feel safe all the time. Information for children and young people

Many families live in fear – the ongoing fear of violence. This can happen when one adult bullies another adult and perhaps other members of the family. It may involve constant hitting, kicking, shouting, threatening, or throwing things.

It can be scary for young people who live in a house where domestic violence is happening. They may have many thoughts and fears:

- I'm afraid to go home.
- Am I the only one this is happening to?
- I'm worried about my Mum.
- I can't concentrate in school.
- Are my friends' homes like this?
- Who can I tell about this?
- Is this my fault?
- What can I do to help?

If there is violence in your home, there are some things you should realise:

- You are not the one this is happening to – domestic violence happens in many families.
- Domestic violence is wrong – no one has the right to hurt another person.
- You are not to blame – domestic violence is not a result of anything you have said or done.
- You do not have to keep this problem to yourself – this article provides information on people and organisations that can help.
- Trust your feelings. If you do not feel safe you can talk to someone about your feelings.

'There is nothing so awful (or so small) that we can't talk about it with someone.'
Protective Behaviours
Network, UK

What is an abusive relationship?

All relationships have their ups and downs. However, these can be worked out by talking to each other and reaching a compromise. Being in a healthy relationship can give you friendship, support, closeness and love. However, there can also be conflict and disagreements. An abusive relationship is often based on fear.

A relationship that has fear in it, is wrong!

Fear may be caused by one person:

- Shouting at or hitting their partner.
- Criticising or putting their partner down.
- Controlling their partner.
- Forcing their partner to do something they do not feel comfortable with.

Why do some people abuse others?

There are many reasons why some people are abusive:

- They have certain ideas about their rights in relationships.
- They regard their partner as their property.
- They deny they have a problem.
- They react to difference in opinion with violence.

It is important to remember that abuse is wrong – behaviour is always a choice with a consequence.

Why would anyone stay in an abusive relationship?

People may stay in an abusive relationship for many reasons. Maybe:

- They've lost touch with friends and have no one to turn to.
- They hope things will get better.
- Their friends all have partners.
- They don't know how to end a relationship.

Leaving any relationship can be a difficult decision to make.

Heading for healthy relationships

The importance of respect

A healthy relationship should be based upon mutual respect for each other. Such a relationship will give importance to:

Rights – paying attention to each other's rights and respecting these.

Equality – giving equal importance to each other's needs.

Sharing – exchanging thoughts, experiences and feelings.

Patience – realising that relationships take effort and time.

Exploring differences – accepting that you are different people. Life would be pretty boring if we were all the same!

Communication – being open and honest with each other and talking things through.

Trust – this is the essential base for any relationship.

Remember!

Getting hurt and feeling scared are difficult things to live with. However, there is a way out, there is help.

There may be someone or some people you know who can help – think of people you could talk to, who you can trust and feel safe with. It may be a family member, a friend, a teacher, a youth leader etc.

Women's Aid can provide help for adults. There are also organisations that can help young people.

Some useful telephone numbers

NSPCC
Helpline 0808 808 5678

ChildLine
0800 1111

Youthline
0808 808 8000

In an emergency phone the police – 999

• The above information is from the leaflet *No fear here!*, produced by Northern Ireland Women's Aid Federation. For their contact details and those of other Women's Aid groups, please see page 41.

© *Northern Ireland Women's Aid Federation*

Domestic violence facts

Information from the Women's Aid Federation of England

Domestic violence worldwide

Domestic Violence extends across all countries and cultures

• Intimate violence is one of the principal factors resulting in health inequalities across gender specifically, and forms a significant barrier to women receiving effective and equal health care, as acknowledged in national and international documents throughout the world. WHO. Factsheet No 239. June 2000.

• Violence against women has serious consequences for their physical and mental health. Abused women are more likely to suffer from depression, anxiety, psychosomatic symptoms, eating problems and sexual dysfunction. Violence may also affect their reproductive health. WHO. Factsheet No 239. June 2000.

• Domestic violence has a major impact upon the health and welfare of women and children worldwide. The 1995 World Development report by the United Nations shows, that on a world scale, it is a significant cause of disability and death. *Domestic*

Women's Aid
FEDERATION OF ENGLAND

Violence and Social Care: A Report on two Conferences held by the Social Services Inspectorate. London: DoH, 1996.

• 5% of health years of life are lost worldwide by women because of domestic violence. *Domestic Violence and Social Care: A Report on two Conferences held by the Social Services Inspectorate.* London: DoH, 1996.

• In a major survey done of over 12,000 Canadian women in 1993, findings showed that one in four women reported experiencing violence from a partner or ex-partner. *The Violence Against Women Survey.* Ottawa: Ministry of Supply & Services, 1993.

• Switzerland 1997 – 20% of a small sample of women report being physically assaulted.

• Korea 1992 – Random sample of

entire country found 38% of wives report physical abuse in the last year.

• Uganda 1997 – Representative sample 41% of women report being beaten or physically harmed by a partner.

• Colombia 1995 – National representative sample of 6,000 19% physically assaulted in their lifetime. WHO. *Violence Against Women: A Health Priority Issue.* July 1997.

General statistics

• Of all crimes reported to the *British Crime Survey 2000* more than 1 in 20 were classified as domestic violence. *The British Crime Survey: England and Wales.* London: Home Office, 2000.

• Domestic violence accounts for almost a quarter (23%) of all violent crime. *The British Crime Survey: England and Wales.* London: Home Office, 2000.

• In 1999 37% of women homicide victims were killed by present or former partners, compared to 6% of men. This totals 92 women, – 1 every 3 days, or 2 women per week. *Criminal Statistics England*

& Wales 1999. London: Home Office, 1999.

- Women are at greatest risk of homicide at the point of separation or after leaving a violent partner. Lees, S. 'Marital rape and marital murder', in Hanmer, J. et al. *Home Truths about Domestic Violence: Feminist Influences on Policy and Practice: A Reader*. London: Routledge, 2000.

- It is estimated that one in four women will experience domestic violence at some time in their lives. *Domestic Violence: a Health Care Issue*. London: BMA, 1998.

- Domestic violence often continues and may escalate in severity after separation. Mirrlees-Black, C. *Domestic Violence: BCS Self-Completion Questionnaire*. London : Home Office, 1999.

- We also know that violence against women and children knows no boundaries of culture, age, sexual preference, body ability, class, ethnicity or creed. Lloyd, S. 'Defining violence against women', in Bewley, S., Friend, J. and Mezey, G. (Eds.) *Violence Against Women*. London: RCOG, 1997.

- 1 in 5 young men and 1 in 10 young women think that abuse or violence against women is acceptable. Zero Tolerance Charitable Trust. 1998.

- Repeat victimisation is common. More than half of all victims of domestic violence are involved in more than one incident. No other type of crime has a rate of repeat victimisation as high. *The British Crime Survey: England and Wales 2000*. London: Home Office, 2000.

- On average a woman will be assaulted by her partner or ex-partner 35 times before reporting it to the police. Yearnshire, S. 'Analysis of cohort', in Bewley, S., Friend, J. and Mezey, G. (Eds.) *Violence Against Women*. London: RCOG, 1997.

- Domestic violence is the least likely violent crime to be reported to the police. The *British Crime Survey 2000* found that just under 1/3 of incidents were reported.

British Crime Survey: England and Wales 2000. London: Home Office, 2000.

- Every minute in the UK, the police receive a call from the public for assistance for domestic violence. This leads to police receiving an estimated 1,300 calls each day or over 570,000 each year. Professor Stanko, E. 'The Day to Count: A Snapshot of the Impact of Domestic Violence in the UK'. *Criminal Justice* 1:2, 2000.

- In any one day nearly 7,000 women and children are sheltering from violence in refuges in the United Kingdom. Women's Aid Federation of England.

- An estimated 19,910 women and 28,520 children stayed in refuges in England in the year ending 31 March 1998. Women's Aid Federation of England, 1999.

- On the 'Day to Count', 200 women asked for safe refuge in England (nearly 300 in the UK) and could not be accommodated in already full refuges. Professor Stanko, E. 'The Day to Count: A Snapshot of the Impact of Domestic Violence in the UK'. *Criminal Justice* 1:2, 2000.

- Over 35,000 women called the Women's Aid National Domestic Violence Helpline this year (2000). Women's Aid Federation of England, 2001.

- The estimated total costs in providing advice, support and assistance for those facing domestic violence in Greater London are £278 million (per year). Professor Stanko, E. et al. *Counting the Costs*. London: Crime Concern, 1998.

- 76% of the children who had

court-ordered contact were said to have been further abused as a result of contact being set up. Radford, L. et al. *Unreasonable Fears*. Bristol: Women's Aid, 1999.

- A 1996 British Crime Survey by the Home Office revealed that 12% of disabled women aged 16-29 had experienced domestic violence in 1995. This compares with 8.2% of non-disabled women of the same age. Mirrlees-Black, C. *Domestic Violence: BCS Self-Completion Questionnaire*. London: Home Office, 1999.

- Nearly 1 in 5 counselling sessions held in Relate Centres in England on 28/9/00 mentioned domestic violence as an issue in the marriage. In Northern Ireland this rose to over 1 in 5. Professor Stanko, E. 'The Day to Count: A Snapshot of the Impact of Domestic Violence in the UK'. *Criminal Justice* 1:2, 2000.

- Weapons are less likely to be used in assaults but victims of domestic violence are more likely to be injured. *British Crime Survey: England and Wales 2000*. London: Home Office, 2000.

• Compiled by Hilary Abrahams of the Domestic Violence Research Group, University of Bristol, and Women's Aid Federation of England.

• The above information is from the Domestic Violence Statistical Factsheet No. 1 from Women's Aid's web site which can be found at w w w . w o m e n s a i d . o r g . u k Alternatively, see page 41 for their address details.

© 2001 Women's Aid Federation of England. All rights reserved.

What is domestic abuse?

Information from Scottish Women's Aid

Domestic abuse is the physical, mental and/or sexual abuse of a woman by someone with whom she is or has been in a relationship. Domestic abuse also affects the children living in the house and there are links between domestic abuse and all forms of child abuse. Physical abuse can include slapping, punching, strangling, using weapons, scalding, burning.

Mental abuse can include humiliation and degradation, keeping the woman from contact with her family and friends, threats against the woman or her children, name-calling. Sexual abuse can include being forced to take part in sex acts against her will, being sexually assaulted with objects, being raped.

Any woman can be abused, there is no 'typical abused woman'. It is likely that we all know women who have been abused. In Women's Aid, we see women from all backgrounds, all ages, all sections of society. Children and young people also experience domestic abuse, either by seeing or hearing their mother's abuse, or by being abused themselves. Research shows that 1 in 4 women experience abuse at some time in their lives. In Scotland, in 2000-2001, Women's Aid groups received almost 60,000 requests for help.

Are you a woman who is being abused?

These are some things that someone close to you could be doing:
- hitting you
- threatening you
- humiliating you
- forcing you to have sex
- threatening the children
- abusing your children
- breaking things in the house
- keeping you short of money
- playing mind games with you
- accusing you of being unfaithful
- ridiculing your beliefs
- isolating you from friends and family

- using contact with the children to abuse you or the children
- keeping your passport and threatening to have you and the children deported

This could make you feel:
- frightened
- degraded
- unable to make decisions
- trapped

Myths and reality

Myth: *'She must deserve it or provoke it.'*
Reality: There is no justification for using violence, unless your life is in

> ### Are you in any way ill-treated or frightened by the man you live with?
> *Bill of Rights for Women*
> - I am not to blame for being beaten and abused
> - I am not the cause of another's violent behaviour
> - I do not like or want it
> - I do not have to take it
> - I am an important human being
> - I am a worthwhile woman
> - I deserve to be treated with respect
> - I do have power to take good care of myself
> - I can decide for myself what is best for me
> - I can make changes in my life if I want to
> - I am not alone
> - I can ask others to help me
> - I am worth working for and changing for
> - I deserve to make my own life safe and happy

danger. No one deserves to be abused, and there is always an alternative, no matter how angry you are.

Myth: *'She must enjoy it, otherwise she'd leave.'*
Reality: Women stay with abusive men for many reasons, but not because they enjoy being abused. They may not know they are entitled to permanent rehousing if they leave home because of violence, and think they would be homeless. They may not know they are entitled to Income Support for themselves and their children, and think they would be penniless. They may fear they would lose their children if they 'desert' their partners. They may not know Women's Aid can provide safe, secret refuge, and fear that they would be found wherever they tried to go. They may feel that it is unfair to take the children away from their father. They may feel the abuse is their fault, and that they do not deserve a life free from violence. Or they may have been told by their partner that he will find and kill them if they try to leave. None of these have anything to do with enjoying being abused.

Myth: *'It's just the odd domestic tiff. Everybody has arguments.'*
Reality: The difference between the occasional argument, which all couples have, and domestic violence is that the latter is quite deliberate behaviour which is used by men to exert power and control over their women partners. A range of different types of controlling behaviours are used, from depriving her of money or sleep, criticising her appearance, telling her who she can be friendly with, locking her in the house, hitting her, pulling her hair, hitting her with weapons, raping her, threatening to kill her and her children.

Myth: *'It's all caused by drink.'*
Reality: Some men only abuse their partners when they have been drinking, but some only do it when

they are sober, and some do it drunk or sober. Drink can provide an easy excuse, but is more of a trigger than a root cause of violence.

Myth: 'It only happens in problem families.'
Reality: Men from all walks of life, all ethnic backgrounds and all ages abuse their women partners. There is no typical abuser, and no typical abused woman. Women's Aid has helped women whose partners were doctors, social workers, ministers, solicitors, psychiatrists. Most of the women who come to Women's Aid for help have no problems in their lives other than those caused by their partner's violence. Once they have escaped from the abuse, most women are as capable of leading a normal life as anyone.

Myth: 'These men must be mentally ill.'
Reality: For a lot of people, it is easier to believe that an abusive man is mentally ill than it is to accept that he knows exactly what he is doing when he assaults, or rapes or tortures his partner. Most men who abuse their partners are only violent to them, never to anyone else. Most men who abuse are able to function normally in society, in the workplace, in all their other contacts with people.

Myth: 'Men who abuse were abused themselves as children.'
Reality: There is no evidence that there is a 'cycle of violence', whereby children who were abused, or who

> *There is no typical abuser, and no typical abused woman. Women's Aid has helped women whose partners were doctors, social workers, ministers, solicitors, psychiatrists*

witnessed abuse, go on to become abusers themselves. Many men who abuse come from families with no history of violence. Many have brothers who are not abusive. Children who witness abuse do not automatically grow up to be violent towards their partners, many completely reject the use of abusive behaviour as a result of their experiences.

Myth: 'It was one-off. He's really sorry, and it won't happen again.'
Reality: Once a man has started to abuse his partner, it is likely to happen again. It is rarely an isolated incident, usually it is part of a pattern of controlling behaviour, which may not have been recognised as such e.g. telling her what to wear, who to see, being very possessive and jealous. Men often say they are sorry afterwards, make promises and say they'll never do it again. Often women who have left return to violent partners because of these promises, and there may be a 'honeymoon' period when he appears

to be the perfect partner. However, most abusers will abuse again, maybe in a different form, and women should be wary of their promises.

Myth: 'Women should stay for the sake of their children. Children need a father.'
Reality: Children who experience domestic violence suffer emotionally and some may also be physically or sexually abused. Many women leave when they see the effects on their children of their partner's abuse. Children's emotional and physical health tends to improve when they come into refuges. Children need love and security, which they can get from their mother, more than they need a 'father figure', especially one whom they know to be abusive to their mother. Some children of abused women do, however, have a good relationship with their father, and want to continue to see him. Access visits can be arranged to allow this to happen. Women and children have a right to a life free from violence for the sake of both the women and the children.

• SWA is funded by the Scottish Office. This information was funded by the Scottish Office Civil Law & Legal Aid Division.

• The above information is from the Scottish Women's Aid's web site which can be found at www.scottishwomensaid.co.uk Alternatively, see page 41 for their address details.

© Scottish Women's Aid

Incidence

Domestic violence accounts for one in 20 incidents reported to the *2000 British Crime Survey*

Domestic violence accounts for one in four incidents of violence reported to the *2000 British Crime Survey*

Domestic violence represents a tenth of the violent incidents reported by men[1]

Domestic violence represents two-fifths of the violent incidents reported by women[1]

1 Chris Kershaw, Tracey Budd, Graham Kinshott, Joanna Mattinson, Pat Mayhew and Andy Myhill (2000) *The British Crime Survey 2000*, London. Home Office Statistical Bulletin 18/00. A copy of this report can be downloaded from the Home Office web site www.homeoffice.gov.uk

Source: *Domestic Violence Data Source*

Prevalence and incidence

Information from Domestic Violence Data Source

In discussion around domestic violence the *prevalence* of abuse is taken to refer to the number of people who have experienced domestic violence either in the last year, or at some point in their lives. The *incidence* of domestic violence refers to the number of times that abuse has occurred, either in the last year or at some point in a person's life.

- Domestic violence accounts for one in 20 incidents reported to the 2000 BCS
- Domestic violence accounts for one in four incidents of violence reported to the 2000 BCS
- Domestic violence represents a tenth of the violent incidents reported by men
- Domestic violence represents two-fifths of the violent incidents reported by women

Prevalence

- Different research studies have tried to estimate the proportion of the population who experience domestic violence each year. These can range from under 1%, up to roughly one in ten of the adult female population. The broad variation is because the studies have been undertaken for different reasons, have used different methodologies, and drawn upon different definitions of domestic violence. There are however similarities in the patterns of physical, sexual, emotional and psychological abuse that they uncover
- The estimates for lifetime prevalence of abuse by a partner or ex-partner tend to cluster closer together, with most studies suggesting that one in four adult women will experience domestic violence at some point in their lives.
- Men also experience abuse within their relationships, but they are less likely to report being hurt, frightened or upset by what has

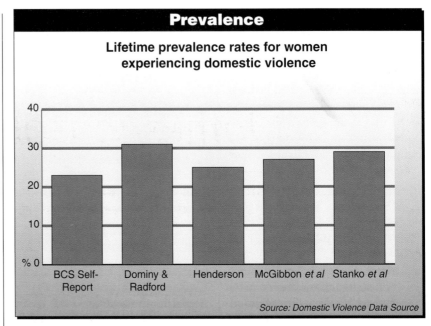

Prevalence

Lifetime prevalence rates for women experiencing domestic violence

Source: Domestic Violence Data Source

happened. They are also less likely to be subjected to a repeated pattern of abuse.

- Research suggests that there are children aged 16 or under in half the households where there is domestic violence. The average number of children per household is two: this means that domestic violence affects the lives of roughly the same number of children as adults within the UK.
- Just under half of people experiencing domestic violence will tell a relative or friend what has happened to them: when applied to the population of England and Wales on a lifetime prevalence estimate, these friends and family represent in excess of 3.6 million people – or one in twelve of the adult population.
- We know something about the prevalence and incidence of domestic violence but we know

---

Just under half of people experiencing domestic violence will tell a relative or friend what has happened to them

---

much less about the proportion of people who are abusive. Mooney found that nearly 1 in 5 men admitted to having used violence against their partner or ex-partner at least once, with only 37% claiming that they would never act violently.

Incidence

- The BCS Self-Report Study estimated that in England and Wales there were 6.6 million incidents of domestic assault in 1995: more than two out of every five resulted in injury. This represents almost one injury every ten seconds, 24 hours a day, 365 days a year.
- The survey also asked about frightening threats (an additional 7 million incidents), but did not include questions about other types of domestic violence. On that basis the figure 13.6 million may be an underestimate: it still represents just under one incident every other second.
- The Day to Count in England, Wales, Scotland and Northern Ireland estimated that an incident of domestic violence occurs within the UK every six to twenty seconds.

- The frequency of incidents gives some insight into the probable levels of demand on key service providers – the following estimates are extrapolations from the BCS as to the likely number of contacts in England and Wales alone:
– Social Services and local Housing Departments will both be contacted following 3% of assaults (roughly one call every 3 minutes, 24 hours a day, 365 days a year)
– after 1 in 10 the victim will get in touch with a nurse or a doctor (roughly one call a minute)
– 1 in 8 domestic assaults will come to police attention (slightly more than one call a minute – this estimate is echoed in the findings from the Day to Count, which monitored the actual demands on the police service for one day)

Please note: Due to space limitations the references for this article have been omitted. A full version of this article including references can be found at www.domesticviolence data.org/4_faqs/faq01.htm

© Domestic Violence Data Source

Domestic violence

Domestic violence does not only affect women, but can have severely damaging consequences for children

Key points
- Barnardo's is committed to zero tolerance of domestic violence against women and children
- Many families live with violence, but this receives less attention than other forms of violence and may be seen by some as a 'normal' part of family life
- Barnardo's works actively to assist parents in finding alternatives to all physical, emotional and verbal violence and aggression
- The impact of domestic violence on children must be fully recognised and treated with greater severity
- In nine out of 10 cases, children are present in the home while violence is going on.[1]
- In about half of cases there is violence to children too.[2]
- Barnardo's campaigns for the abolition of the Defence of Reasonable Chastisement and is seeking the same protection from assault for children as for adults under existing legislation
- Violence within families may go on for years. Children can be at risk of significant harm during this time and the risks can be extremely serious and even life-threatening
- Domestic violence affects children physically, psychologically, emotionally and socially
- More than a quarter of Barnardo's projects are working with families affected by domestic violence

By Lisa Stacey

- Barnardo's believes that the Children Act (1989) should be amended to ensure that un-supervised contact with a child will not be granted to someone who is found to have abused a child.

Background
In November 2000, at the launch of a Government initiative on combating domestic violence, Cherie Booth stated that in England and Wales there is an incident of domestic violence every 26 seconds. Every three days a woman is killed by a former partner.[3] It is thought that one in four women will experience domestic violence at some time in their lives.[4] An estimated 19,910 women and 28,520 children stayed in refuges in England in 1998.[5] Despite this domestic violence often continues after separation and may even escalate in severity.[6]

In 1977, there were around 835,000 reported incidents of domestic violence in England and Wales, 70 per cent against women. This equates to 25 per cent of all violent crime. Since 1981, domestic violence has risen by 187 per cent, but fell 16 per cent between 1995 and 1997. The rise is likely to be related to an increase in reporting.[7]

Only 25 per cent of all domestic violence incidents are reported to the police.[8] In a minority of cases it is

men who have been assaulted by a female partner. However, domestic violence largely concerns violence by men to their female partner or ex-partner. It includes physical, sexual and emotional attacks.

Many people think that domestic violence is an issue that only affects women, yet in 90 per cent of cases, children are in the same or next room while violence is going on.[9] In refuges, 70 per cent of children staying with their mothers had been abused as well.[10] They may be hurt trying to protect their mothers and some, particularly girls, try to keep younger children safe during violent episodes. Between 40 and 60 per cent of all domestic violence cases involve violence to children as well as the mother.[11]

In extreme cases domestic violence can lead to the death of the child or a parent. More than 40 per cent of women killed in England and Wales in 2000/2001 were killed by a current or former partner or lover.[12] Half of all homicide victims in Scotland are killed by their partners.[13]

Many public inquiries into the deaths of children in recent years have shown that the men responsible for the child's death have a history of violence towards their female partners.[14]

Through violence in the home children may suffer emotional and psychological damage. The very young may show physical signs of distress such as bedwetting, stomach aches and sleep disturbances. Children may also suffer 'frozen awareness', where their attention will be focused on the abusing parent. Older children can become very withdrawn or exhibit extreme behaviour as a result of witnessing abuse, and they may feel they are to blame for what is happening. They may become over-protective of their mother, refusing to leave her, which affects their education and social development.[15] Teenage children may become involved in drugs or alcohol; some young people run away from home and others may make suicide attempts.[16]

Women and children fleeing the home as a result of domestic violence are at high risk of homelessness, many having to live in temporary accommodation or refuges. In Scotland, in 1998/9, 9516 children and young people and their mothers or carers, sought refuge in Women's Aid Scotland refuges. Many were turned away because there was no room.[17] In any one day, nearly 7000 women and their children are sheltering from violence in refuges in the UK.[18]

Living in temporary accommodation has its own problems for children. They may suffer emotional effects, including feelings of isolation from friends and family and their education and health could well suffer due to lack of continuity.[19]

For many families, issues of race, culture and religion can add to the difficulty of escaping domestic violence. If they have to move to escape violence, children will have to cope with a new home in a new area, a new school and leaving family and friends behind. They may spend long periods in temporary accommodation, with damaging consequences for their development. Despite the violence, they may still love and miss their dad.

What the Government is doing

Currently there is a Report to the Lord Chancellor's Department on Contact between Children and Violent Parents, which contains proposals for good practice guidelines in dealing with contact applications in cases of domestic violence. Research found 76 per cent of children who were ordered by courts to have contact with a violent parent were said to have been further abused as a result of contact being set up.[20]

Over recent years there have also been a number of cases where children have been murdered during unsupervised contact. These include

---

Many people think that domestic violence is an issue that only affects women, yet in 90 per cent of cases, children are in the same or next room while violence is going on

---

the case of Daniel Philpott aged seven and his three-year-old brother Jordan, killed by their father during an unsupervised visit in August 1999. The contact was granted even though the father was facing charges of threatening to kill his ex-partner.[21]

Barnardo's believes that the Children Act (1989) must be amended to include a rebuttable presumption that unsupervised contact will not be granted to someone who is found to have abused a child, unless the court is satisfied that the child is safe. This provision could also be added to the Adoption and Children Bill. This would allow the court an opportunity to ensure that a thorough risk assessment is carried out before unsupervised contact is granted.

Current legislation

Protection for women and children has been strengthened since the implementation of Part IV, Family Homes and Domestic Violence, of the Family Law Act 1996, which deals with rights to occupy the matrimonial home, occupation orders and non-molestation orders. It also includes amendments to the Children Act 1989 concerning interim care orders and emergency orders, where guardians ad litem are expected to be appointed.

However, Barnardo's is still concerned that children are being exposed to risk. One of our specialist projects in this field, the Phoenix Project, is particularly concerned that some abusing male partners may be using their contact with their children as a way of tracing the woman – and possibly continuing the abuse.

Barnardo's is currently lobbying to use the Adoption and Children Bill as a way to amend the Children Act – to further protect children. This would also point to a need for contact centres (where separated parents can see their children on neutral ground) to be alert to the risks of abusing parents exploiting their visiting rights.

What Barnardo's is doing

Sixty-seven of Barnardo's 300 services report direct work with families and young people affected by domestic violence. A 1996 audit of Barnardo's projects found that 42 per cent reported domestic violence as an issue, with one-fifth saying it was a frequent part of their work. More than a quarter were offering support for affected children.

Barnardo's aims to alleviate the long-term effects of domestic violence on children through counselling and family support services. Many mothers continue to provide love and stability for their children in very difficult circumstances, and Barnardo's aims to strengthen their ability to cope. Where the mother's ability to look after her children has been undermined by the stress of living with fear, we try to help them improve their confidence and self-esteem so that they can protect themselves and their children from violence.

Some projects offer group programmes to help women make plans to tackle what is happening to them, giving them the chance to meet others in the same situation and encouraging them to take control of their lives.

Projects also offer practical help, such as advice and information on housing, financial and legal issues. There is counselling for children to help them talk through their feelings and experiences, together with play sessions, after-school clubs, holidays and outings.

Barnardo's does a small amount of work with men who have been violent towards their partners, with the aim of helping them to change their behaviour, and develop their approach to personal relationships and being a father.

Together with the NSPCC and the Bristol University Domestic Violence Unit, Barnardo's has produced a training pack, *Making an Impact – Children and Domestic Violence*,[22] which is aimed at raising

awareness of the impact of domestic violence and equipping people who work with children with the skills and knowledge to support children through a deeply traumatic time.

The *Making an Impact* pack was published by the Department of Health and distributed to local authorities and other agencies by them. Currently, supplements to the *Making an Impact* material are being produced to take into account the Human Rights Act, the Data Protection Act, legislative developments in Northern Ireland and Scotland, and new research which has, for example, made links between animal abuse and domestic violence.

References

1   NCH (2000) *Factfile* 2001. NCH.
2   Hughes, H M et al (1989) Witnessing spouse abuse and experiencing physical abuse: a 'double whammy'? *Journal of Family Violence* 4(2) p187.
3   Woolf, M (2001) Cherie Booth backs drive to combat domestic violence. *Independent* 29 November.
4   British Medical Association (1998) *Domestic violence: a health care issue*. BMA, 1998.
5   Abrahams, H (2001) Women's Aid Federation of England: domestic violence statistical factsheet number 1.
6   Mirrlees-Black, C (1999) *Domestic violence: findings from a new British Crime Survey self-completion questionnaire*. Home Office.
7   Mirrlees-Black, C et al (1998) *The British Crime Survey: England and Wales*. Home Office Statistical Bulletin 21/98.
8   NCH (1999) *Factfile* 2000. NCH.
9   NCH (2000) *Factfile* 2001. NCH.
10 Bowker I H et al (1988) On the relationship between wife beating and child abuse, in K and Bograd, M (eds) *Feminist perspectives on wife abuse*. Sage.
11 Hughes (1989) As before.
12 Home Office (2001) *Criminal Statistics: England and Wales 2000*. Stationery Office.
13 NCH (2000) *Factfile* 2001 Scotland. NCH.
14 O'Hara, M (1995) Child deaths in the context of domestic violence. *Childright* 115 Apr pp 15-18.
15 NCH (1994) *The hidden victims: children and domestic violence*. NCH.
16 Mullender, A (1996) *Rethinking domestic violence: the social work and probation perspective*. Routledge.
17 NCH (2000) *Factfile* 2001 Scotland. NCH.
18 Abrahams, H (2001) As before
19 Barnardo's (1995) *Doing time: families living in temporary accommodation in London*. Barnardo's.
20 Radford, L et al (1999) *Unreasonable fears*. Bristol Women's Aid.
21 NSPCC (2002) Briefing on the Adoption and Children Bill (2001/2): Part 2: Amendments to the Children Act (1989). NSPCC.
22 Hester, M et al (1998) *Making an impact: children and domestic violence*. Barnardo's. This is available through Barnardo's.

© *Barnardo's*

A few home truths about domestic violence

Domestic violence – more common than street violence

- 1 woman in 4 (some claim 1 in 3) has experienced domestic violence.[1]
- 86% were slapped or punched, 63% were strangled, 61% kicked, 61% struck with an object, 83% had bruises or black eyes, 50% had cuts, 23% had broken bones, 40% had been to hospital for their injuries.[2]
- Almost half (46%) were forced by their partner to have sex, 23% were 'raped with threats', 18% 'raped with violence'.[2] 1 in 7 of all married women are raped by their husbands.[3]
- Almost half of all homicides of women are by a partner or ex-partner. About 100 women are killed in this way in Britain each year, or two every week.[4]
- 4 out of 10 single mothers who had lived with the child's father said that quarrels had led to physical violence.[5]
- Medical studies report that between 1 in 10 and 1 in 5 pregnant women are violently attacked by their partners during the pregnancy.[6]
- A woman rings Women's Aid somewhere in Britain every $2\frac{1}{2}$ minutes every day of the year.[7]
- The risk of suffering domestic violence is the same for women of all ethnic groups.[8]

Children suffer harm and untold distress

- In up to 90% of cases the children witnessed their mother being attacked. In 45-70% the father inflicted violence on the children as well as the mother.[9] 10% of the mothers were sexually abused in front of their children. 27% of the partners had also assaulted the children, including sexually.[2]
- 86% of mothers said there were long-term effects on their children: 1/3 said the children

Women Against Rape

became violent and aggressive, including towards their mother; 31% developed problems at school; 31% had low-self-esteem.[2]

Most violence is not reported, and not acted upon when reported

- Up to 98% of domestic violence is not reported to police.[10] 2 out of 3 mothers told no one at first. The average time before telling someone is 1 to 2 years.[2]
- For 70% of mothers it was hard to tell professionals about children's problems caused by violence. 81% felt guilty; 74% feared the children would be taken away.[2]
- On average it takes 35 assaults before a case comes to court.[11]

  There is little systematic recording or monitoring of domestic violence. Sanctions against violent men are so weak as to protect them. Even in Islington, with a project called 'Domestic Violence Matters' in police stations:
- 58% of incidents were no-crimed (i.e. not recorded as an offence).

- Only 26% of all cases and 63% of 'crimed' (recorded) cases led to an arrest.
- Even in cases where there were visible injuries and the perpetrator was present, arrest occurred in only 45% of cases. [12]

No money, nowhere to go

- 4 out of 5 women raped by their husbands are trapped by lack of resources: no money and nowhere to go.[3]
- Nearly two-thirds of Britain's homeless women are living on the streets because they have been the victims of domestic violence.[13]
- More than 50,000 women and children flee their homes each year to seek shelter in refuges but up to three-quarters find there is nowhere to go.[14]
- 59% of women who leave abusive partners return to them owing to lack of suitable accommodation.[15]

Child Support Act has increased violence against women and children

- Single mothers on Income Support are forced by the CSA into contact with children's

fathers to get maintenance; risking violence against them and their children. 75% of single mothers refuse to co-operate with the CSA because of 'harm or undue distress'. 66% of mothers left their relationship because of concern about the effects of violence on their children.[2]

- Even then, courts almost always award child contact to fathers. Out of 46 cases where fathers were granted contact, only in 7 were provisions made to prevent further abuse. [16]
- Police have said they want no part in moves to verify single mothers' claims that they fear reprisals from ex-partners if they co-operate with the Child Support Agency. Met. Police Cmdr. Kendrick told MPs that police intervention could be 'extremely dangerous' for women and would 'not assist the situation'.[17]

References

1 *The Hidden Figure: Domestic Violence in North London*, Jayne Mooney, Middlesex Univ., 1993 found 1 in 3 experience domestic violence, even excluding cases where women are raped by their partners, subjected to mental cruelty, threatened, grabbed, shaken or pushed. A British Medical Association report, *Domestic Violence, a Health Care Issue*, 1998 found one in four experienced domestic violence, including rape. In the 1996 *British Crime Survey* 23% of women had been assaulted by a partner.
2 *The Hidden Victims, Children and Domestic Violence*, NCH Action for Children, 1994.
3 *Ask Any Woman, a London inquiry into rape and sexual assault*, Ruth E. Hall, Falling Wall Press, Bristol 1985.
4 Homicide statistics 1998.
5 *Lone Parents, Work and Benefits: the first effects of the CSA to 1994*, DSS report No. 61, HMSO, 1997.
6 *Guardian Weekend*, 1 May 1999; *Independent on Sunday*, 5 Dec 1999.
7 *The Guardian*, 20 Oct 1998, p 8.
8 *British Crime Survey 1996*.

Nearly two-thirds of Britain's homeless women are living on the streets because they have been the victims of domestic violence

---

9 *Domestic Violence: A Health Care Issue?*, BMA, 1998.
10 For an overview of estimates, see *Domestic Violence*, Loma J. F. Smith, Home Office Research and Planning Unit, HMSO 1989 p 7.
11 Home Secretary Jack Straw; *The Guardian*, 3 June 1999, p 9.
12 *Domestic Violence Matters: an Evaluation of a Development Project*, Research Findings No. 91, Home Office 1999.
13 *The Independent*, 1 Jun 1999, p 8 (Centre for Housing Policy, Univ. of York).
14 *The Guardian*, 8 Jan 2000, p 12 (Homerton College, Cambridge).
15 Campaign Against Domestic Violence.
16 *Domestic violence and child contact arrangements in England and Denmark*, Marianne Hester and Lorraine Radford, Univ. of Bristol, 1999. The 46 cases were in England.
17 *The Guardian*, 6 Jun 1996.

Women Against Rape

A grassroots multi-racial women's group, established in 1976. The research for this article has been done mostly by unwaged volunteers. Our other work includes pressing for justice, protection, compensation and other resources for all survivors of rape and sexual assault, including racist sexual assault and domestic violence.

- The above information is from a factsheet produced by Women Against Rape. See page 41 for their address details.

© *Women Against Rape*

Key facts

Prevalence
- up to one in ten women experience domestic violence each year, one in four will experience this type of abuse at some point in their lifetime
- there are variations between estimates according to definition of domestic violence used, and also according to methodology. However, the similarities uncovered are more notable than the differences, particularly in relation to the estimates for lifetime prevalence
- men also experience abuse by their partners and ex-partners, but in general they are less likely to report being hurt, frightened or upset by what has happened. They are also less likely to be subjected to a repeated pattern of abuse
- domestic violence also impacts on a survivor's children, their friends and their family
- research suggests that 1 in 5 men may have used violence against their partner or ex-partner at least once.

Incidence
- An incident of domestic violence takes place in the UK every six to 20 seconds
- In England and Wales, approximately every 10 seconds someone is injured as a result of domestic violence
- The frequency of incidents gives some insight into the probable levels of demand on key service providers.

- The above information is an extract from the Domestic Violence Data Source web site which can be found at www.domesticviolencedata.org

© *Domestic Violence Data Source*

The impact of domestic violence

Information from Domestic Violence Data Source

Where individuals are subjected to domestic violence the perpetrator can often employ a range of behaviours, with physical assaults overlapping with psychological, emotional and/or financial abuse. Research has suggested that in some cases the psychological abuse experienced may have a more lasting impact than the injuries sustained, and that this can be true even where those injuries were severe.

He stopped me from going out with my friends. I was restricted to seeing my parents once a week . . . and most of the time he was there in case I said anything about him wrong or anything.[1]

The data presented in this table are taken from the *2000 British Crime Survey*,[2] and show people experiencing domestic violence are more likely to be affected by what has happened to them than for other types of crime. In addition, the extent to which they are likely to be affected tends also to be greater.

The physical, legal, economic and physiological consequences of domestic violence vary from individual to individual.[3] However, the nature of the relationship between the perpetrator and their victim means that the context of any individual incident is generally very different to that of other offence types. Survivors of domestic violence are more likely to have been subjected to a repeated pattern of physical abuse than victims of other types of violence; they are also more likely to experience injury.[2]

People experiencing domestic violence are more likely to be upset than for other types of offences; they are more likely to be afraid and to have difficulty sleeping than people who have been burgled.

Research has estimated that there are 880,000 adults stalked in

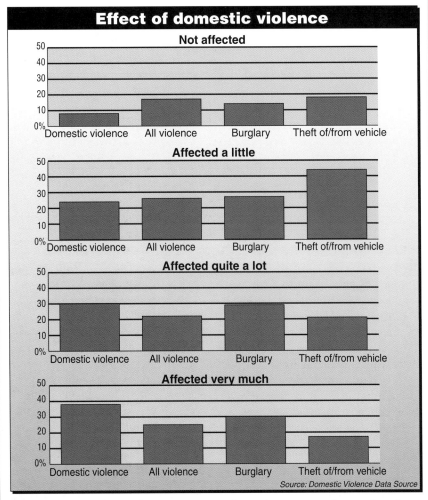

Effect of domestic violence

Source: Domestic Violence Data Source

England and Wales each year: in 3 out of every 10 cases the person doing the stalking is an ex-partner, and in nearly three-quarters of these cases the focus of the persistent and unwanted attention is a woman.[4] Roughly 70% of those stalked reported that they had altered their lifestyle as a result of their experiences: by avoiding people or

---

Domestic violence has a more wide-reaching impact than the person experiencing abuse

---

places, by going out less, or by taking additional personal security measures.

Domestic violence has a more wide-reaching impact than the person experiencing abuse: their friends and family will also be affected:

'I saw a lot when I was growing up and promised myself I would never go through what my mum went through.'[3]

There are also debates around the extent to which witnessing domestic violence as a child may make individuals more likely to find themselves in abusive relationships when they are older, either as a survivor or as a perpetrator (sometimes referred to as the cycle of violence). Recent studies have questioned whether there is in fact any such link[5] – in any event it should be remembered that not all those who are abused grow up to use violence in their relationships, and not all perpetrators of domestic violence witnessed similar abuse as children.

References

1 Nicky Dominy & Lorraine Radford (1996) *Domestic Violence in Surrey: developing an effective inter-agency response* London Roehampton Institute

2 Chris Kershaw, Tracey Budd, Graham Kinshott, Joanna Mattinson, Pat Mayhew & Andy Myhill (2000) The *British Crime Survey 2000* London Home Office Statistical Bulletin 18/00. A copy of this report can be downloaded from the Home Office Web site: www.homeoffice.gov.uk

3 Betsy Stanko, Debbie Crisp, Chris Hale & Hebe Lucraft (1998) *Counting the Costs: estimating the impact of domestic violence in the London Borough of Hackney* Swindon Crime Concern

4 Tracey Budd & Joanna Mattinson (2000) *Stalking: findings from the 1998 British Crime Survey* London Home Office RDSD Research Findings No. 129. A copy of this report can be downloaded from the Home Office Web site: http://www.homeoffice.gov.uk

5 Martie P Thompson, Linda E Saltzman & Holly Johnson (2001) Risk Factors for Physical Injury Among Women Assaulted by Current or Former Spouses *Violence Against Women* Vol 7 No 8 August 2001.

● The above information is an extract from the Domestic Violence Data Source web site which can be found at www.domesticviolencedata.org

© Domestic Violence Data Source

Study to find true cost of domestic violence

By Lucy Ward, Political Correspondent

The government is to carry out the first survey of the multi-million pound cost to the economy of domestic violence, which claims the lives of two women a week.

The Cabinet Office minister Barbara Roche, announcing the move today at a meeting of EU women's ministers in Spain, has ordered the research in an effort to gauge the severity and impact of the crime, paving the way for further steps to address it.

The study, which Ms Roche believes will reveal 'quite startling figures', is expected to assess a broad range of costs such as medical care for victims, policing and legal bills, and the cost of days lost from work through injury or stress.

Campaigners arguing for more funding to address domestic violence, which accounts for a quarter of all violent crime, hope the study's conclusions will convince ministers to channel more money into prevention and victim support.

Ms Roche, a barrister with experience of domestic violence cases and a long-held interest in the issue, has been influenced by research by Betsy Stanko, who found that domestic violence cost £278m of public money a year in London alone. Her study did not include factors such as hospitalisation and trials, making the true total much higher.

The government research, to be conducted by the women and equality unit, will seek evidence from domestic violence experts, police and leading economists. It will also involve trade unions and business representatives to assess the impact of domestic violence on the workplace.

The government is committed to addressing domestic violence, having published the first national strategy on the issue, Break the Chain, in 1998. Some campaigners feel the issue has since failed to gain the promised profile.

© Guardian Newspapers Limited 2002

Children and domestic abuse

Information from Hidden Hurt

Children are often described as the 'forgotten victims' of domestic abuse. Children are affected not only by directly witnessing abuse, but also by living in an environment where their mother – usually the main caregiver – is being repeatedly victimised. Children in a home where the mother is being abused are also at greater risk of being abused themselves, or being used to control their mother. Due to his own lack of self-worth the abusive partner feels the need to control all those to whom he considers himself superior. In a family, this includes the children.

Witnessing abuse

Children witness violence in the home in a number of different ways. They may see or hear the abusive episode, be used or even involved in the violence (e.g. the child may be in his mother's arms when she is hit), will experience the aftermath, and sense the tension in the build-up to the abuse. Even when the parents believe the children were unaware of what was happening, the children can often give detailed accounts of the events. As well as the physical violence often found in abusive relationships, the children will almost certainly be subjected to frequent emotional abuse of the mother in the form of name-calling, accusations and threats made by the abuser in their presence. As mentioned above, where the wife/partner is being abused, the children are also likely to be abused themselves. This is most true of emotional abuse, where the children's own self-esteem is battered by being shouted at, told they are stupid or are not trying hard enough, or given mixed messages by being favoured one moment and put down the next. Quite apart from possible physical involvement or direct abuse, these emotionally damaging actions have a detrimental and often long-lasting effect on the children.

The effect of witnessing abuse

Many children who witness the abuse of their mothers demonstrate signifi-

> *Even when the parents believe the children were unaware of what was happening, the children can often give detailed accounts of the events*

'People throw around statistics saying that up to 70 or 80% of children of batterers are also abused. That statistic is wrong. EVERY child who witnesses abuse is a victim of abuse. As an abused child, and then as an adult trying to recover, I was far more affected by witnessing the abuse of my mother than I was by the abuse directed toward me.'

Carlita

cant behavioural and/or emotional problems including psychosomatic disorders, stuttering, anxiety and fears, sleep disruption, excessive crying and problems at school.

How your child or children will be affected depends on the individual child, their age and gender, how much they witness and whether or not they are personally involved in the abuse, their personality and support available to them. Although research in this field is still largely lacking, it is generally agreed that domestic violence or abuse is highly relevant to the child's present and future well-being, and that there is a significant overlap with child abuse.

In brief, children may experience any of the following problems:

Emotional problems

Crying, anxiety and sadness, confusion, anger (which can be directed toward either parent or other children, etc.), depression, suicidal behaviour, nightmares, fears and phobias. In younger children and babies eating and sleeping disorders are common. Children can also suffer from PTSD (Post-Traumatic Stress Disorder).

Behavioural problems

Aggression, becoming troublesome at home or at school, withdrawing into or isolating themselves, regressive behaviour (such as baby-talk, wanting bottles or dummies, etc.), lower academic achievements.

Physical problems

Bed-wetting, nervous ticks, headaches or stomach aches, nausea or vomiting, eating disorders, insomnia.

Older children will often hold themselves responsible for the abuse, especially where extreme violence has been an issue. Children living in an abusive environment may also condone violence or the threat of violence to resolve conflict in relationships.

It has to be remembered that even in situations where the child is either not targeted directly with abuse or is 'only' witnessing abuse, it can lead to very serious psychological trauma with possible long-term effects, affecting not only the child's well-being during or shortly after the abuse, but affecting the child's ability to build and maintain healthy relationships in his/her adult life.

• The above information is from Hidden Hurt's web site: www.hiddenhurt.co.uk Alternatively, see page 41 for their address details.

© Hidden Hurt

Domestic violence gives warning of child abuse

Information from the NSPCC

Abused children come mainly from families where there is domestic violence and other serious family problems. This is a key finding from a new NSPCC report into child maltreatment, published today (Sunday 24 February 2002).

Child Maltreatment in the Family is the second report from the most comprehensive research into child abuse and neglect ever undertaken in this country. It presents the findings of a survey of childhood experiences of 2,869 18-24-year-olds, carried out by BMRB International for the NSPCC FULL STOP Campaign.

The first report showed physical abuse was the most common form of child maltreatment, with seven per cent of young people reporting serious physical abuse at the hands of parents and carers, including being hit with a fist or implement, beaten up, burned and scalded. The new findings show:

• An overwhelming eight out of ten of the young people who had suffered serious physical abuse had also experienced domestic violence. For nearly half (43%) of these, the domestic violence was constant or frequent.

• Almost nine out of ten young people who said they had been

NSPCC ●
Cruelty to children must stop. FULL STOP.

neglected also reported some domestic violence, though this dropped to around six in ten of those assessed as seriously neglected by the researchers.

In all, 21 of the 27 young people (78 per cent) who reported sexual abuse by their parents also reported domestic violence – in nearly all cases a constant or frequent occurrence. Previous NSPCC research and the vast majority of studies on domestic violence illustrate that by far the most common and serious form of violence is from men to women. NSPCC child protection work supports the finding that domestic violence increases the risk of abuse to children, now revealed in a broader sample.

In all, 78 per cent of the young people who reported sexual abuse by their parents also reported domestic violence

Most children do not experience maltreatment in their families. But when they do, the research revealed strong links between child maltreatment and other family relationship problems, particularly where parents are distant and children have no respect for them. The study also found children experiencing frequent changes in family structure were especially vulnerable to abuse.

Those who had grown up in lone-parent or broken families were three to six times more likely to have suffered serious abuse, though some abuse may have preceded family breakdown.

The study shows that child maltreatment often occurs in otherwise stable and loving families, but is likely to be less serious, less frequent and less long-lived. There is however a significant minority of children who suffer repeated, pathological abuse by parents and carers, who experience poor family relationships, lack of warmth and constant criticism.

In all, five per cent of children experience more than one type of serious maltreatment by parents. These children are likely to suffer years of multiple maltreatment, telling no one and receiving little help or comfort. Their situation is dire.

Mary Marsh, Director and Chief Executive of the NSPCC, said: 'The terrible levels of child cruelty revealed in this report are not inevitable. It is vital that members of the public and child protection professionals, including the NSPCC, work effectively together to reach out to abused children who have no one else to turn to. Every action counts.

'Violence between adults caring for a child can sound a warning bell that a child is at risk of serious maltreatment. We must all be alert to the ways in which destructive family relationships can damage a child and act on any concerns that a child is at risk of abuse. Some danger signals to watch out for are children who are frequently dirty or hungry, constantly "put down", insulted or humiliated or afraid of parents or carers.

'This study reveals how some parents maltreat their children when faced with serious problems and stress. We can help prevent children from coming to harm by ensuring adequate help and support is available to vulnerable families – particularly when experiencing difficulties such as domestic violence, relationship breakdown, stress, money and health problems.'

As part of its FULL STOP Campaign the NSPCC has set up 29 domestic violence projects around the UK to provide help and counselling for parents and families in difficulty. The charity is also developing and strengthening a range of services including Young People's Centres that listen to children and respond to their needs. Anyone with concerns about a child can contact the NSPCC National Child Protection Helpline on 0808 800 5000.

• *Child Maltreatment in the Family* (priced £15) was written by Pat Cawson, Head of Child Protection Research at the NSPCC. The first report *Child Maltreatment in the UK* (priced £23), published November 2000, established definitions of child maltreatment and provided figures for the prevalence of child abuse and neglect. The reports aim to help the NSPCC and others develop strategies to prevent child maltreatment and plan effective child protection services. They are available from the NSPCC Publications & Information Unit, 42 Curtain Road, London EC2A.

Domestic violence is a general term to describe a range of behaviours often used by one person to control and dominate another with whom they have, or have had, a close family relationship. In most cases the relationship will be between current or former partners; the abuser will be male and the victim female.

Crown prosecution service (2001) *Domestic Violence: Policy for Prosecuting Cases of Domestic Violence.*

• The above information is from an NSPCC press release from their web site which can be found at www.nspcc.org.uk Alternatively, see page 41 for their address details.

© NSPCC 2002

A case study from the NSPCC

After suffering years of physical and emotional abuse by her partner, Ms G contacted an NSPCC domestic violence project. She was very concerned because her two children, an 18-month-old girl and a boy aged eight, were traumatised after witnessing a recent violent assault on her by their father.

Despite being granted an injunction against her partner, Ms G felt depressed and overwhelmed by the abuse. She felt incapable to help her children recover from the trauma as both were suffering from nightmares and other emotional and behavioural disturbances. Ms G's confidence as a mother was severely undermined and it was beginning to affect her relationship with her children.

One of the most difficult issues for Ms G was that her husband had sought to undermine her by encouraging the eight-year-old, Simon, to copy his own abusive behaviour against Ms G. After the father left home, her son blamed her for making him go and he became even more hostile towards her. He became aggressive towards his school friends and sometimes appeared very sad.

The NSPCC worked with Ms G initially to relieve her of the blame and guilt which so many women in her situation feel. She also needed to understand the impact of domestic violence on herself and the children. Eventually she felt strong enough to try and establish a better relationship with Simon. The project supported her as she reassured him that he was not responsible for the abuse and gradually his aggressive outbursts diminished.

While the project continued to support Ms G with her young daughter, it was felt that Simon was ready for individual therapy. This was helpful for him as he now felt he could talk openly about the violence. It became clear that he had witnessed far more than his mother had realised and that he had also been directly abused. These concerns were passed on to the Social Services Department while Ms G also sought appropriate legal advice regarding the children's contact with their father.

Simon continued to receive help from the project, to build up his self-esteem and ensure that he didn't feel responsible for the abuse. The project used an ecomap, a pictorial representation of different parts of Simon's life, to help him talk about his nightmares, home and school life and how he felt about himself and the significant people in his life. Through this, Simon showed that he was still experiencing difficulties at school and also that he hated the fact that his Mum smacked him. Recognising the damage she had suffered from being hit herself, Ms G readily accepted different strategies for disciplining Simon that wouldn't destroy his confidence further. Simon then asked for his mother and sister to join some of his sessions and as a family they were able to play together.

© NSPCC 2002

The truth about domestic violence

Information for women who are or have experienced domestic violence

- Domestic violence includes physical, emotional and sexual abuse.
- Domestic violence is totally unacceptable. Every woman has the right to live her life free of violence, abuse, intimidation and fear.
- Domestic violence is very common. One woman in four experiences domestic violence at some point in her life.
- Domestic violence is very dangerous. Each week in the UK, two women are killed by a partner or ex-partner.
- Domestic violence is not just about individual men abusing individual women. It is also about the systematic abuse and oppression of women in the society in which we live.
- Domestic violence is about power and control. Abusive, violent and sexually abusive behaviour is wide-ranging and subtle in what it tries to achieve.
- Domestic violence is intentional and instrumental behaviour. It is about scaring you into doing something that you don't want to do or out of doing something that you do want to do.
- The abuser is 100% responsible for his abuse. His abuse is his problem and his responsibility.
- It is not your fault. No woman deserves to be abused, regardless of what she says or does.
- A man can change. His behaviour is within his control and he can choose to stop.
- You can't change him. He himself is the only person who can stop his violence.
- We can't change him. If he attends DVIP's Violence Prevention Programme there is no guarantee he will change – some men do, but many don't.

- He may change a bit. Men do sometimes change a bit, maybe becoming less violent, but remaining abusive and intimidating. You can decide for yourself whether he has changed enough.

Domestic violence is about power and control. Abusive, violent and sexually abusive behaviour is wide-ranging and subtle in what it tries to achieve

- You don't have to put up with it. A woman has the right to safety and respect, to put herself and her children first and to focus on her needs.
- You can increase your safety. If he is intent on being violent, you will not be able to stop him, but there might be things you can do to increase your safety.

• The above information is an extract from the Domestic Violence Intervention Project's web site which can be found at www.dvip.org

© Domestic Violence Intervention Project

Power and control

VIOLENCE

USING COERCION & THREATS
Making and/or carrying out threats to do something to hurt her • threatening to leave her, to commit suicide, to report her to welfare • making her drop charges. • making her do illegal things.

USING INTIMIDATION
Making her afraid by using looks, actions, gestures . . . smashing things • destroying her property • abusing pets • displaying weapons.

USING ECONOMIC ABUSE
Preventing her from getting or keeping a job • making her ask for money • giving her an allowance • taking her money • not letting her know about or have access to family income.

USING EMOTIONAL ABUSE
Putting her down • making her feel bad about herself • calling her names • making her think she's crazy • playing mind games • humiliating her • making her feel guilty.

USING MALE PRIVILEGE
Treating her like a servant • making all the big decisions, acting the 'master of the castle' • being the one to define men's and women's roles.

POWER AND CONTROL

USING CHILDREN
Making her feel guilty about the children • using the children to relay messages • using visitation to harass her • threatening to take the children away.

MINIMISING DENYING AND BLAMING
Making light of the abuse and not taking her concerns about it seriously • saying the abuse didn't happen • shifting responsbility for abusive behaviour • saying she caused it.

USING ISOLATION
Controlling what she does, who she sees and talks to, what she reads, where she goes • limiting her outside involvement • using jealousy to justify actions.

Hitting home

Domestic violence and young women

Domestic violence is one of the most common violent crimes in the UK. The latest statistics indicate that one in four women will experience domestic violence during their lifetime[1] and every week two women are killed by current or former partners.[2] The majority of domestic violence victims are women. A recent snapshot survey revealed that 81 per cent of domestic violence calls to the police were made by women attacked by men.[3] There is no such thing as a typical domestic violence victim. Research evidence suggests that any woman regardless of race, culture, nationality, religion, sexuality, disability, age, class or education level is at risk.[4]

What is domestic violence?

The 1993 Home Affairs Select Committee defined domestic violence as: 'Any form of physical, sexual or emotional abuse which takes place within the context of a close relationship. In most cases, the relationship will be between partners (married, cohabiting or otherwise) or ex-partners.'

Behind closed doors

Domestic violence may be life-threatening, systematic and long term. It can occur anywhere but most frequently it happens behind closed doors, away from the public eye and unknown to anyone outside the immediate family. Far from being a safe haven, a place of comfort and security, the home can be a place of danger, terror and injury. Research shows that women are far more at risk of violence from men in their family or with whom they have a close relationship than from male strangers. Out of around 48,000 women who contacted Rape Crisis Federation groups during 1998, 97 per cent were abused by men they knew.[5]

Young women at risk

Research suggests that young women are at significant risk of domestic violence. Twenty-eight per cent of women aged 20-24 had experienced domestic assault at some time in their life and 13 per cent of women aged 16-24 said they had been assaulted by a partner within the last year,[6] Where domestic violence was the cause of a visit to hospital, 16-25-year-olds made up nearly half of attendances.[7]

The causes of domestic violence

Gender inequality

Dobash and Dobash (1979)[8] found that the four main sources of conflict that lead to violent acts are: 'Men's possessiveness and jealousy, men's expectations concerning women's domestic work, men's sense of the right to punish "their" women for perceived wrongdoing, and the importance to men of maintaining or exercising their position of authority.'

Social acceptability of male violence

Historically, the law placed women under the authority of men (husbands or fathers) and legitimised the use of physical punishment to control them. These laws no longer exist but many of the underlying beliefs and attitudes about male dominance and superiority remain.

It is a shocking reality that male violence against women is still seen by many as normal and acceptable, even by young people. A major national research study into young people's attitudes to violence, sex and relationships found that one in two boys and one in three girls thought

> *Far from being a safe haven, a place of comfort and security, the home can be a place of danger, terror and injury*

that there were come circumstances when it could be acceptable to hit a woman or to force her to have sex.[9] More recent research reiterates the high tolerance levels of young people towards violence and abuse: 19 per cent of young women did not think being forced to have sex is rape.[10]

Why are young women at risk?

There are a number of factors that make young women especially vulnerable to violence and abuse.

Pregnancy and young motherhood

Pregnancy often triggers domestic violence or exacerbates a pre-existing problem.[11] Reported rates of physical, sexual or emotional violence by a partner during pregnancy are as high as 20.2 per cent.[12]

The post-natal period is also a time of high risk.[13] Adolescent women are particularly vulnerable: two studies have found higher rates of domestic violence among pregnant teenagers than among older women.[14, 15] Other factors which are associated with teenage pregnancy such as low educational achievement, poor self-esteem and lack of employment opportunities have also been linked to higher rates of abuse.[16]

Economic status

Research has demonstrated that women who work outside the home are at lower risk of violence than women who do not.[6] Women with young children are more likely to be at home than older women whose children have reached school age. These younger women are therefore more likely to be financially dependent on their partner, accentuating the power imbalance and making it very difficult to escape a violent relationship on which they and their children depend for food and shelter.

Dating relationships

In a recent study, four out of five

young women reported having experienced at least one kind of harassment/abuse. Focusing on the more serious incidents – sexual assault, forced to have sex and physical assault by a partner – almost twice as many young women as young men reported these experiences (28 per cent to 15 per cent).[10] Young women frequently report feeling under pressure or forced to have sex and often lack the confidence and negotiating skills to resist unwanted sexual advances.

Family violence
In addition to partner/boyfriend inflicted violence, young women may be subjected to violence and abuse from the extended family. The experience of extended family violence has been found to be particularly acute for some young married Asian women. Interviews with a number of Pakistani women who have suffered domestic violence reveal that violence from their husbands was at best ignored and at worst instigated and encouraged by their mother-in-law or sisters-in-law.[17] Young Asian women may feel particularly trapped in violent and abusive relationships, as they risk shame and dishonour, social isolation and even deportation if they leave their husbands. Women affected by the 12-month rule are not eligible to claim state benefits which means they are excluded from refuges and unable to seek legal protection.

The effects of domestic violence

Domestic violence has serious, long-term effects on young women's health. Women who have suffered abuse are more likely to suffer from depression, anxiety, psychosomatic symptoms, eating problems and sexual dysfunction. Violence may also affect their reproductive health.[18] Domestic violence in pregnancy can cause miscarriage, premature birth, low birth weight, foetal injury and foetal death. As a coping mechanism, women are more likely to abuse alcohol or drugs. As well as experiencing the painful effects of physical injury, the long-term psychological damage can lead

to severe mental health problems including depression, self-harm and attempted suicide. As many as 50 per cent of women receiving psychiatric services have experienced sexual or physical abuse.[19]

Young women frequently report feeling under pressure or forced to have sex and often lack the confidence and negotiating skills to resist unwanted sexual advances

---

References
1 Greater London Authority (2001) *The London Domestic Violence Strategy*.
2 Home Office (1998) *Homicide Statistics*.
3 Stanko B (2000) The Day to Count: A Snapshot of the Impact of Domestic Violence in the UK. *Criminal Justice* 1:2.
4 Home Office (2000) *Multi Agency Guidance for Domestic Violence*.
5 Rape Crisis Federation statistics (1998)
6 Mirrlees-Black C (1998) *Domestic Violence: findings from a new British Crime Survey self-completion questionnaire*. Home Office Research Study 192. Home Office.
7 Department of Health (2000) Conference Report: *Domestic Violence: A Health Response: Working in a Wider Partnership*.
8 Dobash R and Dobash R (1979) *Violence Against Wives*. The Free Press New York and Macmillan Distributing.
9 Burton S et al (1998) *Young People's Attitudes Towards Violence, Sex and Relationships*. Zero Tolerance Trust
10 Regan L and Kelly L (2001) *Teenage Tolerance, The Hidden Lives of Young Irish People*. Dublin Women's Aid.
11 Mezey G and Bewley S (1997) *Violence Against Women*. Royal College of Obstetricians and Gynaecologists.
12 O'Campo P (1994) Verbal abuse and physical violence among a cohort of low-income pregnant women. *Women's Health Issues*: 4:29-37.
13 Hedin L (2000) Postpartum, also a risk period for domestic violence. *European Journal of Obstetrics and Gynaecology and Reproductive Biology* 89: 41-45.
14 Parker B et al (1993) Physical and emotional abuse in pregnancy: a comparison of adult and teenage women. *Nurs Res* 42:173-8.
15 Gazmararian et al (1995) The relationship between pregnancy intendedness and physical violence in mothers of newborns. *Obstet Gynecol* 85: 1031-8.
16 Stewart D (1993) Physical abuse in pregnancy. *Can Med Assoc J* 149: 1257-63.
17 Choudry S (1996) *Pakistani Women's Experiences of Domestic Violence in Great Britain*. Research Findings no 42. Home Office.
18 World Health Organisation (2000) Factsheet number 239.
19 Williams J et al (1993) *Purchasing Effective Mental Health Services for Women: A Framework for Action*. University of Kent/Mind Publications.

• The above information is an extract from *Hitting home: Domestic violence and young women*, a briefing produced by YWCA. See page 41 for their address details or visit their web site at www.ywca-gb.org.uk
© YWCA 2002

'The thing is, I still love her'

For six months, Daniel Hoste was repeatedly beaten up by his girlfriend, often for such minor transgressions as keeping his shoes on inside. It was only after he left her that he realised his experience was far from unusual

Imagine being punched in the face by a stranger, then beaten about the head with a phone so hard that it cracks. Next, they start to strangle you. The reason for this abrupt attack is that you've left a door open. Now imagine that instead of the attacker being a stranger it is the person you love, someone who mostly returns your love in abundance.

I don't have to imagine a situation such as this. It happened a dozen times to me over a six-month period and the reality was severely bruised ribs, about 50 bumps and bruises, a black eye, bloody lips, and scratches and bites so severe they bled. I was also threatened with a baseball bat, an empty beer bottle and had a full one thrown at my head. The emotional abuse was much worse: the physical marks have healed; my mental scars will never go away. The other thing worth mentioning is that I'm a man.

I am an athletic 6ft 1in; my ex-girlfriend is a petite 5ft 4in. Aggressive fights I have seen between men in pubs were nothing compared to the frightening rage I saw when she hit out. I feel that her punches were cast with more than 20 years of hurt, guilt, shame and anger. Hurt people hurt people.

I ended up sleeping in my car; wearing the same clothes for a fortnight; couldn't work; drank so that I was ill; got in debt; lost friends, my sex drive, my self-esteem and much of what I owned, and some of what I kept she ripped or smashed.

I am an athletic 6ft 1in; my ex-girlfriend is a petite 5ft 4in. Aggressive fights I have seen between men in pubs were nothing compared to the frightening rage I saw when she hit out

---

Now aged 33, I have had three long-term relationships and have barely even had arguments in these. Friends describe me as laid-back, and the last fight I had was two decades ago in the playground. Several people said I was the last person to whom they thought it would happen. I loved life until this started; by the end I was so numb that I wanted to jump off a cliff. I wouldn't have felt a thing.

We met working and soon started to spend every day together. After six weeks we went away for a few days, and told each other that we had fallen in love.

Those days in the initial months were the most beautiful I've had. We'd eat out, take long walks together; I'd present her with sweet-smelling lilies and she'd sing our love songs to me. The only warning sign was the sheer intensity of it: her attention to intricate details such as the way my freckles fell on my arms or that her favourite colour was the very same shade of purple I liked. And she wanted love more than anyone I've ever met.

But I couldn't do enough for her, and if I went to work, she'd tell me that I thought more about money than her. If I went to the newsagent's, she'd tell me to pull my jersey round my bum or girls would be looking at it. I thought this was outrageously cute and that she really loved me. Now I see that it was obsession, not devotion. She rejected my friends for various reasons. My flat was rejected too, as I'd lived there with an ex, and she never wanted to meet my family – and so my isolation started.

Her mood swings became increasingly unpredictable, so after three months I stopped seeing her. But I couldn't stop thinking about the romantic times and our passionate sex, so we met up after a week. She invited me back to her flat and all was Hollywood movies once more – until we stepped through her door. She accused me of not caring about her home because I'd left my shoes on, so I apologised and took them off. Suddenly she was punching me. I protected my head as best I could. When I heard my nose crunch I knew it was time to leave.

The next day she called, full of remorse, so we made up. By now some friends had told me that I was in an abusive relationship, but that idea was too ridiculous to contemplate: I thought only white-trash women were abused by snarling ex-jailbirds. Still, friends and my family would tell me to leave, that she was destroying my life, but then we'd have our gorgeous days again and I'd think, 'How can I?'

I was hit only when she was drunk. I was verbally abused whenever she felt down. 'You have a strong character' became 'You're not a real man,' and 'This is the best sex I've known' became 'No woman would want to fuck you.'

Soon, she who could make me the happiest person could also make me feel like unlovable scum. So when I was hit, as she told me, I deserved it. If only I could not be so tired and stay awake all night with her and do the shopping, cleaning, DIY, cooking, and earn more and spend more time with her and drive her everywhere but not drive so badly, and tell her something interesting and listen to her more and be like her ex (who had left one day without saying bye after four months) and always be there for her and get out when she told me, she wouldn't get angry with me. Soon the eggshells were so scattered that it was difficult to walk anywhere.

When the boundaries of verbal abuse had been nudged, those of physical abuse kicked in, but always behind her closed door. It didn't matter what the 'reason' was in the end. Once it was for telling a joke she didn't find funny. Again I must stress the blurred anger I saw, more like a starving, rabid dog ravaging some raw meat than a human being. Why didn't I leave? Because most of the time our love affair was gorgeous.

She was kind, shy and vulnerable, or at least portrayed herself that way. I thought she'd been a victim, and I'd be the hero to save her. I was also chasing the high that we'd had, had nowhere to go, and felt really alone: I could talk to some male mates about it, but most couldn't relate to what I was saying. Even when I went to casualty about my ribs, I lied about how it had happened.

I never hit back and the only marks she suffered were bruises on her arms from where she'd hit me so hard. I had to get away because I was going to kill myself, or kill her. When she threatened me with a baseball bat, I grabbed it and for a split second I was going to strike her. I believe we would have both been in institutions of one kind or another if I hadn't dropped it and walked away.

I had to learn how to be alive again. I called counsellors for the first time and read about abusive relationships. I realised I had been in an abusive relationship: I read familiar things: 'sleep deprivation', 'belittling', 'threats', 'manipulation'. I also read that many abusers have personality disorders, particularly borderline personality disorder (BPD).

When I looked at the checklist of nine characteristics of BPD, of which five have to be present for the condition to be diagnosed, I emphatically ticked eight. It was as though sunlight had shone on me for the first time.

There's ample literature and helplines for domestic violence victims, but mostly for women. I read that many abusers were abused themselves; it is a vicious cycle. I learned that when I crossed an intimacy line I most likely reminded her of someone from childhood, probably an adult care-giver who might have been overpowering, neglectful or abusive. One counsellor had no doubts: 'I wonder who she was punching when she hit you?'

The more I confessed to close male friends, the more I heard that

She who could make me the happiest person could also make me feel like unlovable scum. So when I was hit, as she told me, I deserved it

some of them had been abused by their female partners. In some ways I'm glad it happened. While she was clearly a very unwell person (which is why I'm writing this anonymously), I was obviously not a well-balanced person. If I hadn't stayed there she couldn't have abused me.

So I am dealing with why I had low self-esteem, admitting that I am stubborn and compulsive, and that I'd rather have had a dysfunctional relationship than no relationship. I am scared of having a new relationship, but I know one will come along and it will be better for this experience.

I'm taking care of myself and I'm writing a novel about it, which is great therapy. Also, I've become involved with ManKind, a new organisation set up to help men with relationship problems. I wouldn't want anyone – male or female – to suffer a second of what I went through. More men are becoming victims and we need to change attitudes, allow men to talk, get rid of this taboo. If you are in an abusive relationship, walk away now. Look after yourself. You deserve it .

As for my ex-partner, I hope she has sought help. I've had no contact with her for some time, and when I think of the abuse it seems increasingly distant. I'm still working out what happened for her to have such rage: genes, ex-boyfriends, an abusive care-giver or a combination of these? I may never know. But when I hear certain songs, or smell lilies, or visit places where we had brilliant times, I feel overwhelmingly sad. Thing is, I still love her, but how can I?

• You can contact ManKind on 01643-863352. Daniel Hoste is a pseudonym.

© *Guardian Newspapers Limited 2002*

Domestic violence: is the law letting women down?

It's a cowardly, despicable crime committed in thousands of households across Britain every day. Its victims are bruised and battered – often beyond recognition – and many fear for their lives. But in nearly all cases the police are powerless to act. Why are women still at risk?

Her nose is bloody and the bruises are just about to show when she answers the front door. Sharon has clearly been the victim of a serious assault but the two police officers just look weary rather than shocked as they follow her into her living room.

Her assailant won't be difficult to find. There he is, standing next to the sofa, still smelling of drink, still angry, and only slightly wary in the presence of the forces of law and order.

He has little to fear, though. The two policemen make no move to arrest him. They've been to this house many times before and seen this scenario, or one very like it, acted out again and again.

SHE DOESN'T WISH TO PRESS CHARGES...

By Steve Tooze

One of the office turns towards the trembling, tear-stained woman and asks her gently but firmly, 'Are you going to press charges this time, love? If you don't, you realise there's nothing we can do to help you?'

Sharon sneaks a frightened glance at her attacker, glowering menacingly from the other side of the room, and whispers, 'No, I can't.'

He'll be back

As they've done many times before, the policemen take her assailant by the arm and lead him outside.

Sharon knows the routine by now. Her husband will disappear for an hour or two but she also knows he'll be back. Maybe he'll beg forgiveness, maybe he'll beat her again. She'll just have to wait – alone and in fear.

As the door closes, she hears one of the policemen say to the man who has just bloodied her nose and blacked her eyes, 'I know women can be difficult, mate, but you've got to learn to control your temper.'

Horrifyingly, these disturbing events are not unique. This type of violence is repeated daily in hundreds of homes throughout Britain.

Unbelievable, if the man who attacked Sharon had been a total stranger she'd met in the street, the police would have prosecuted automatically and without question. Instead, she was attacked in the supposed safety of her own home and her attacker was her husband – a man who is supposed to love her.

Sharon's ordeal is part of a distressing pattern where thousands of battered women are denied proper protection by the law because of a still deep-seated belief that a beating in the home is not as serious as an attack on the street.

A terrible danger

Julie Brindle, a law reform expert at the University of North London, has no doubt that some of the current attitudes toward domestic violence actually make life easy for the abusers. 'Sadly, in many parts of this country, a man giving a woman a slap is still not seen as a proper crime,' she says. 'It's seen as a private matter, a row between husband and wife, where the law should only get involved as a last resort.

'In reality, the men who carry out these attacks are a terrible danger. In too many cases, domestic violence can often escalate into murder.'

National statistics back up her fears. Figures for homicides in the UK in 1998 show that two women were killed every week in England and Wales by their own partner or ex-partner.

Further recent reports make frightening reading. A study carried out in Hackney, east London, in 1997, discovered that one in nine women is severely beaten by their partner every year. And in 1999, a national study showed that almost a quarter of women will be the victim of a domestic assault in their lifetime.

And that may only be the tip of the iceberg. Just one in three domestic assaults resulting in injury is ever reported to the police, according to the 1996 British Crime Survey.

Julie is in no doubt about how to drastically reduce the appallingly high number of assaults carried out on women by their partners.

'The police should prosecute them immediately and without hesitation,' she says firmly. 'Show them that their violence is socially unacceptable. That would deter most men from raising their fists to their wives or girlfriends.

'It should not be left up to individual police officers or forces to decide that an assault which takes place in the home is a domestic, a private matter between man and his wife.

'And it certainly shouldn't be left up to the woman who has been assaulted to decide whether or not her partner is taken to court. It should be an automatic process that police always implement.'

However, a change in attitude by prosecutors would have to be backed up by tougher sentences being handed out by magistrates and judges.

'Forget conditional discharges, probation and counselling,' Julie says. 'Those are the sorts of sentences which should be handed out for stealing sandwiches from Marks & Spencer.

'The courts should be jailing men who hit their partners in the same way they would a man who assaults a woman in the street.'

Vicious attack

Julie feels that a change in attitude by judges and magistrates would send out a strong message to the rest of society, making domestic violence as unacceptable as drink-driving – which, 20 years ago, was seen as harmless fun.

'Studies show, for example, that juries are often of the opinion that it's almost understandable if a man hits a woman who nags him,' she says. 'That's because the way the law deals with domestic violence encourages people to see it as an extension of a marital tiff, rather than what it actually is – a vicious attack by a stronger person on a weaker one.'

That same attitude by prosecutors and courts often puts women in danger, even after they've found the courage to leave the man who's been beating them.

'Court injunctions ordering the man to stay away from the woman's home usually offer no protection at all because they are not enforced vigorously enough by the police,' says Julie.

'The man can only really be arrested if he is found somewhere on or around the premises when the police arrive. But many police forces don't treat calls to enforce injections.'

There are indications, though, that the Government, police and the courts are gradually starting to tackle the enormity of the problem in this country

---

'Court injunctions ordering the man to stay away from the woman's home usually offer no protection at all'

In March last year Home Office minister Paul Boateng produced a 10-point plan to encourage courts, police and social services to develop across-the-board strategies to tackle domestic violence.

The Government also announced it had earmarked £7 million within its crime reduction programme to fund a 'violence against women initiative'.

Mr Boateng praised schemes such as the Killingbeck Repeat Victimisation Model – piloted by West Yorkshire Police – in which officers must take action at the scene of a domestic attack. There, police use steadily tougher measures against an attacker each time they are called back to a particular home

Individual forces, such as the Metropolitan Police, have developed sympathetic new methods to deal with domestic violence. Scotland Yard's Specialist Domestic Violence Unit has received national praise as, 'absolutely brilliant and progressive' by women's support groups.

Long way to go

But Sandra Horley, Chief Executive of Refuge, which provides homes and shelter for abused women, firmly believes that the UK still has a very long way to go to match the groundbreaking and vastly expensive anti-domestic violence initiatives launched in some other countries.

The Canadian federal government, for example, recently provided $136 million (£62.7 million) funding for a massive multi-agency programme to ensure that violent husbands are arrested and prosecuted, that police, judges and the general public are re-educated and re-trained, and that abused women and their children are given support and protection.

Initial studies indicate this co-ordinated response has reduced attacks on women by their partners by up to 25%.

Similarly, the US government has poured $3.3 billion (£2.3 billion) into a nationwide programme, providing $825 million (£582 million) for a national telephone helpline, and $975 million (£688 million) to train police and judges in a new, sympathetic approach to battered women.

In stark contrast, Refuge is struggling to raise £2.2 million to keep its network of homes up and running.

'There are promising initiatives but they're very patchy and the situation can vary hugely from one region to another,' says Sandra Horley. 'The Government needs to provide a lot more money across the board to make a real difference.'

Sandra wants a National Domestic Violence Task Force set up to tackle the problem of overhauling the nation's health, education and criminal justice systems.

'A friend called me recently after she'd been battered by her partner in front of her young children,' she says. 'She didn't even realise that it was a crime for her husband to hit her.

'And when the police arrived they asked her what she wanted them to do. She was too frightened to press charges, so they just left her alone – without medical help or support.'

The Criminal Prosecution Service is often reluctant to take men to court when their partner won't press charges because they fear the women will undermine the case by refusing to give evidence. 'Our experiences show that's not what happens,' Sandra says.

'A battered woman feels empowered and supported when she realises that the choice of whether or not to press charges is taken out of her hands. A woman will give evidence if she is given the right support and protection.'

It's time the law stepped in and sent out a strong message to all violent men stressing that it is utterly unacceptable to beat a partner. That is not happening right now. Until it does, many women's lives are still in jeopardy.

• The above article first appeared in *Woman's Own*, June 2001.

© Steve Tooze, Woman's Own

Victims of domestic violence

Two case studies

Wendy

Wendy Finnegan, 32, a mum of three, was beaten and terrorised by her husband, Paul, throughout their eight-year relationship. She now runs SAFE, a support group for battered women, and lives happily with a new partner.

Paul raped me only one. I count myself lucky. Lots of battered women are sexually abused on a regular basis as well as being beaten and humiliated.

Paul was a charming rogue I fell in love with at 15 and married when I was 21. It was that love and my own lack of self-esteem that kept me with him when the beatings began.

He almost always hit me for the same reason – because he was insanely jealous. He was convinced I slept with every man I came into contact with, no matter how much I denied it.

He broke my nose on two occasions, once by very calmly and coldly headbutting me in the face after accusing me of sleeping with a guy from work who I hardly even knew.

I tried fighting back when he hit me. But that only made the beatings worse. One time he threw me on the floor and repeatedly kicked me in the head. Several times he threw me down the stairs.

On another occasion, he smashed me so hard against an old-fashioned telephone box I had bruises in the shape of the windows all over my back.

He was arrested once when he punched me in the street in front of two policemen in a car because I refused him money. He was wearing a heavy signet ring and it ripped my bottom lip to pieces. It took 30 stitches to put it back together.

I didn't press charges. I was too scared and he always charmed me and made me believe it was my fault for answering him back. Also, I still desperately wanted to keep my family together.

After a while, the violence started to seem normal. I developed a high tolerance to the pain and didn't think anything of being covered in bruises. That was how my life was and I just accepted it.

The way the police dealt with it didn't help. They would come to the house and say, in front of Paul, that it was my decision whether or not to take him to court.

Sometimes I'd say I wanted to press charges. But then I'd start worrying about losing my home and my family and I'd be frightened of what he'd do as revenge. So I'd always withdraw my complaint.

I'm sure the violence would have stopped right at the beginning if Paul had been charged with assault.

I didn't have the confidence to do it myself. I desperately wanted somebody to take it all out of my hands and stop him. Instead, the police would take him out of the house like a naughty boy, tell him to leave me alone for a few hours, then drop him at the end of the road.

I felt the legal system didn't take the beatings seriously. It was as if everyone thought I was stupid for bothering them and stupid for not pressing charges. It made me feel it was useless to call them for help.

I only realised how different the approach could have been after I'd divorced Paul and then cancelled plans to re-marry him. He came to the house, accused me of sleeping with someone else and then punched me in the face, breaking my nose for a second time.

This time the police were brilliant. Paul was arrested and went on the run when he was released. Police officers called round regularly to make sure I was okay and gave me an alarm and a mobile phone. It made such a difference.

Paul was eventually imprisoned for six months for assault after he attacked me again and was CS gassed by the police after locking himself in the house with my sons.

I've since moved away from the area and started a new life with a partner who couldn't be more gentle and loving. But I just wish Paul had been prosecuted years ago and saved me years of fear and violence.

• *Woman's Own* legal adviser Peter Smith explains: 'There is a new Home Office initiative which tries to remove the pressure on victims of domestic violence. However, it has always been difficult for the police to prosecute without the evidence of the partner who has been beaten.'

• Contact SAFE on 07714 783278.

Elizabeth*

Elizabeth, a 40-year-old executive PA and a mum of a nine-year-old son, was beaten by her former boyfriend for three years.*

The police were completely useless at stopping my boyfriend from hurting me. They would arrive, usually after a complaint from their neighbours about all the screaming and crashing as he hit me around. I was usually too terrified to call them myself.

I'd be scratched and bruised and bleeding when I answered the door and one of the PCs would ask me, 'What would you like us to do?'

My boyfriend would be standing right behind me. I'd be hurt and frightened and so, of course, I'd say, 'Nothing.' And they'd say, 'Okay. If you have any more problems, give us a call.'

Then they'd take my boyfriend outside and tell him to calm down and pop down the pub for an hour or two so I could 'tidy myself up'. Sometimes he would come back, calm and apologetic and begging for forgiveness. Other times, he'd be furious and threatening, ready to hit me again. I'd be left, alone and scared, to guess which it might be this time.

My boyfriend was the perfect loving partner until I was four months pregnant with our son. His own childhood had made him very insecure and distrusting of women and he became convinced that out baby would eventually replace him in my affections.

One day he was shaving and discovered his aftershave was finished. He suddenly turned round to me and said, 'You'll be too concerned with looking after that brat to buy me any more.' Then he slashed my arm open with his razor.

He was beside himself with regret afterwards, apologising and begging me to forgive him. He said it would never happen again. I forgave him. But, of course, that was only the start of the beatings.

He slapped, kicked and punched me throughout my pregnancy. He only stopped a month or so before the baby was born, then he started again when the baby was still tiny.

It always followed the same pattern. For a few days, he would buy me flowers and jewellery and continually tell me he loved me and that he would never hurt me.

Then there would be a period of tension. He'd be silent, moody and ultra-picky about everything I did. I'd be shaking with fear, scurrying around trying to defuse the situation.

Finally, he'd find some excuse to lose it completely. I remember him pulling our bed to one side, finding the carpet a bit dusty and shouting, 'When was the last time you vacuumed under here?'

One time he hit me for not having all the tins lined up the right way in the cupboards. On another occasion, it was for not cooking his shepherd's pie the way he liked it.

He'd scream abuse at me. Tell me I was fat, ugly and useless until he'd worked himself into enough of a temper to start hitting me. My poor little son would be cowering in another room, listening to his mum being beaten.

He used his fists, his head and his feet. Once he beat me with a dog chain. Another time he hit me so hard on my shins with a broom handle that it broke in two.

Another time he grabbed something off a shelf and threw it at me. I don't know what it was because it happened so quickly, but it cut off my earlobe. And once I was ordered to stand in a corner naked for hours as punishment for something so minor that I can't remember what it was.

My nose was broken twice and my jaw once. My body was often covered in bruises, although he always took enormous care not to leave marks on my arms and legs where they would show.

At first I would run away to my parents or to friends. But then he hounded and terrorised them too. He'd ring at 3am and snarl at them, 'Can you smell petrol? You will soon.' In the end, they became too frightened for their own safety to shelter me.

His constant verbal abuse and violence reduced my confidence and self-esteem to zero. I believed what he said. I must be a useless, fat slag no one else would ever want.

I had a young child and literally nowhere else to turn. So I would listen to his promises that he'd changed, that he'd never hit me again and I'd go back to him.

He almost wrecked my career too. I was a secretary and he'd ring and ring my office, begging me to forgive him or threatening me. Eventually my boss would suggest that I take some time off and sort out my personal life.

I made him leave several times and took out a court injunction ordering him to stay away from the house. But he just ignored the injunction and came round to terrorise me.

I'd call the police but they wouldn't treat it as a priority because they'd been there so often. By the time they arrived he would already have gone and they'd say they couldn't do anything unless they actually caught him on the premises.

Eventually I went to a refuge where, at last, I was told that I wasn't doing anything wrong, that it was his problem and I shouldn't be the one dealing with it. That's when I realised the only way I was ever going to escape from him was to lose everything – my job, my home, my whole life.

I waited until he was in a drunken stupor one night and crept out of the house with my son. I was so screwed up at the time that I remember seriously thinking about killing him by smashing him over the head with a rolling pin. Thankfully I realised I just didn't have it in me to go through with it.

I went to a city on the other side of the country. It took me four years to rebuild my life. But I've been happily living with a new partner for the last two years and, at last, I feel that I've been able to put the whole nightmare behind me.

It could all have been so different if the police had automatically prosecuted him right at the start. I was the victim, not him, and therefore the last person who should have been allowed to decide whether or not he was prosecuted.

They should have treated him like any thug who hit a woman in the street and charged him with assault – regardless of whether I wanted them to or not.

I'm convinced it would have stopped him hitting me again if he had been taken to court and imprisoned the first time the police came to our home.

Instead, the police treated it as a domestic row between a woman and her partner – and so he got away with hitting me for years.

* Elizabeth does not wish to reveal her real name.

• The above stories first appeared in *Woman's Own*, June 2001.
© Steve Tooze, Woman's Own

Break the chain

Information from the Home Office

What you can do about domestic violence

If you are being physically or sexually assaulted by someone you live with, or are being threatened by them, that is domestic violence. Domestic violence is controlling behaviour and includes all kinds of physical, sexual and emotional abuse within all kinds of intimate relationships. It harms women and men. It wrecks thousands of lives.

Domestic violence is rarely a one-off event. Physical and sexual abuse tends to increase in frequency and severity over time, sometimes only ending when one person actually kills the other. Other forms of abusive or controlling behaviour may be ongoing. This chain of events needs to be broken.

A lot of people can help to break the chain. Some of the organisations working to do this are mentioned in this article. But individuals also have an important part to play. For people experiencing violence, the support of a trusted friend can be invaluable. Breaking the chain is a job for everyone.

Domestic violence is much more common than most people realise. Even if you are not experiencing it yourself, you may well know someone who is. This article may help you to help them.

We must not let domestic violence beat us. Together we can break the chain.

What can I do?

If you are in a violent relationship there are three steps you can take.
- Recognise that it is happening to you
- Accept that you are not to blame
- Seek help and support

Recognising domestic violence

Domestic violence includes all kinds

of physical, sexual and emotional abuse within all kinds of intimate relationships. The most harmful abuse is carried out by men against female partners, but abuse can also occur by women against men and within same-sex relationships.

People experience domestic violence regardless of their social group, class, age, race, disability, sexuality and lifestyle. The abuse can begin at any time – in new relationships or after many years spent together.

Domestic violence can take a number of forms such as physical assault, sexual abuse, rape, and threats. In addition, it may include destructive criticism, pressure tactics, disrespect, breaking trust, isolation and harassment. Some abusers offer 'rewards' on certain conditions, or in an attempt to persuade their partners that the abuse won't happen again. However persuasive they seem, the violence usually gets worse over time.

Accepting that you are not to blame

It is not easy to accept that a loved one can behave so aggressively. Because they can't explain their partner's behaviour, many people assume that they themselves are to blame. They are not. No one deserves to be assaulted, abused or humiliated, least of all by a partner in a supposedly caring relationship. It is the abuser's behaviour which needs to change: there is no excuse.

Seeking help

The most important thing you can do is to tell someone. For some the decision to seek help is quickly and easily made. For many, the process will be long and painful as they try to make the relationship work and stop the violence. The prospect of leaving an abusive relationship can be as frightening as the prospect of staying. Most people try to find help a number of times before they get what they need, and even after leaving there may still be a risk. Never be afraid to ask for help again.

In an emergency, always call the police by dialling 999 (minicom 0800 112 999).

Who can I talk to?

If you or someone you know are

experiencing or have experienced domestic violence, there are a range of organisations that can help. Some useful addresses and telephone numbers are provided here, but there are many others: libraries, local authorities and Citizens' Advice Bureaux are good sources of further information.

Women's Aid National Domestic Violence Helpline
0345 023 468

This service can give you support, help and information. They will discuss the practical and legal options available, and if you wish refer you to a local Women's Aid refuge and advice service, or other sources of help. All calls are taken in strictest confidence. The helpline is open from 10am to 5pm Monday to Thursday and from 10am to 3pm on Fridays. Outside these hours you can contact your local Women's Aid service through the local phone book, or access the Women's Aid website (www.womensaid.org.uk). In Wales you can also call Welsh Women's Aid on 029 20 390874.

Local Women's Aid refuge services
There are nearly 300 local refuge projects in England and Wales. Many local Women's Aid groups also run advice centers, drop-in centres or outreach services to more isolated areas, as well as local helplines. You can call in to see someone, or telephone for advice and support, without having to stay in a refuge.

Refuge 24-Hour National Crisis Line
0990 995 443

This service provides information, support and practical help, 24 hours a day, 7 days a week, to women experiencing domestic violence. It can refer women and their children to refuges throughout the UK.

Men's Advice Line and Enquiries
020 8 644 9914

Information, support and advice to men experiencing domestic violence. Open from 9am to 10pm, Monday and Wednesday. Local projects for men are available in some areas.

Victim Support
0845 30 30 900

Victim Support offers information and support to victims of crime, whether or not they have reported the crime to the police. All help given is free and confidential. You can contact Victim Support direct, or ask the police to put you in touch with your local group. The national helpline is open from 9am to 9pm Monday to Friday and from 9am to 7pm on Saturdays, Sundays and Bank Holidays.

Shelterline
0808 800 4444

Emergency access to refuge services.

The Police
Many kinds of domestic abuse are criminal offences, and the police take all domestic violence very seriously. Most forces have specially trained, experienced officers who will listen and speak to you separately from your partner. Women can ask to be seen by a woman officer. The police can, if you wish, arrange medical aid, transport and a safe place for you to go. Their first priorities are your safety and well-being and, if applicable, the safety and well-being of your children.

To contact the police in an emergency, dial 999. At other times, you can contact your local police station. You can find the number in your telephone directory.

National Health Service
Many people do not realise how direct an impact their partner's behaviour can have on their health and that of their children. They may experience depression and anxiety which are often just as damaging as physical injuries – or more so. This can happen during the relationship, or after it has finished.

Talk to your GP or health visitor and tell them the real cause of your worries and injuries. If you have to go to casualty, try to be open about the reasons. This is vital if you are to get the proper medical help and support you need. Remember: you can always talk to NHS staff in confidence.

The Samaritans
0345 90 90 90

24-hour confidential emotional support for anyone in crisis. The number given above links up all their branches; or you can use the number of your local branch, which you will find in your phone book.

National Child Protection Helpline (NSPCC)
0800 800 500
minicom: 0800 056 0566

This free, confidential service for anyone concerned about children at risk offers counselling, information and advice.

Careline
020 8514 1177

A national confidential counselling line for children, young people and adults on any issue including family, marital and relationship problems, child abuse, rape and sexual assault, depression and anxiety.

Relate
Relationship counselling, for non-emergency situations. There will be a local number in your phone book.

How can I protect myself from the violence?

Legal protection
Whether or not the police use the criminal law against a violent person, you can still use the civil law to get protection to allow you to live in safety. Under the Family Law Act 1996, many people experiencing domestic violence can apply for court orders against their abusers. For example, you can apply for an order against someone you live with or have lived with (whether or not you have been married), someone you have agreed to marry, or someone with whom you share parental responsibility for a child.

These orders can stop the abusive behaviour itself, or in some cases prevent the abusive person from entering the home. Courts can attach a power of arrest so that if the order is not obeyed, the abuser can be taken to court by the police.

If you are on income support or have a very low income you may be able to get legal aid to pay for a solicitor's advice and legal proceedings.

You can find out more from the police, a solicitor, your local magistrates' court or county court, Citizens' Advice Bureau or Women's Aid group.

Moving away

If you are abused by the person you live with, or someone connected with you such as an ex-partner, you may decide it is best to leave your home. If you have nowhere else to go, you may wish to consider contacting the helplines given in this article or the housing department of your local council. The council should provide a 24-hour emergency homelessness service. If they consider that you are vulnerable because you are at risk of domestic violence, and that it would not be reasonable for you to continue living at your home, they must help you to find somewhere else to live. If so, they may provide you with temporary accommodation such as a place in a hostel, bed-and-breakfast hotel or women's refuge.

A refuge is a safe house where women and children can live free from violence. It offers a temporary breathing space where decisions can be made free from pressure and fear. There are refuges specifically for women and children from particular ethnic or cultural backgrounds – for example black, Asian, Latin American or Jewish women – and some refuges have disabled access and staff trained in special needs.

One of the reasons that many people stay on in abusive relationships is because they wonder how they will manage financially if they leave. There are various benefits which you may be able to claim and some can be paid even if you are working. Your local Social Security Benefits Office will be able to advise you.

What about the children?

There are established links between domestic violence and child abuse. Children may themselves be injured or abused or may be at risk of accidental injury, and they may also suffer indirectly even when not directly abused themselves: they are often more aware of the abuse than their parents realise.

Some abusers threaten that if their partner leaves or tells anyone about the violence, their children will be taken away from them. Social services will not take children away for this reason. If you fear your partner will abduct the children, you should

seek advice. Your local Women's Aid group, Law Centre, Citizens' Advice Bureau, or a solicitor can advise on issues such as parental responsibility, where children should live, who they should have contact with, changes of school and related problems.

How can I help a friend who is experiencing domestic violence?

Unless the person you are trying to help has been very open about their experiences it may be difficult for you to acknowledge the problem directly. However, if someone does confide in you that they are experiencing domestic violence, there are some basic steps that you can take:

- Be understanding. Explain that there are many people in this situation. Acknowledge that it takes strength to trust someone enough to talk about the abuse. Allow them time to talk, and don't push them to give too much detail if they don't want to.
- Be supportive. Say that no one deserves to be threatened or beaten, despite what the abuser may have said. Be a good listener, and encourage them to express their hurt and anger.
- Let them make their own decisions, even if this means they aren't ready to leave the relationship. This is their decision.
- Ask if they have suffered physical harm. Offer to go along with them to hospital if they need to go. Help them to report the assault to the police if they choose to do so.
- Provide information, as far as you can, on the help which is available. Explore the options to-

gether. Go together to visit a solicitor if the person is ready to take this step.
- Plan safe strategies for leaving the abusive relationship, letting them decide what is safe and what is not. Don't encourage them to follow any strategies that they are expressing doubt about.
- Offer the use of your address and/ or telephone number for information and messages.
- Above all, look after yourself while you are supporting someone else. Do not put yourself in a dangerous position: for example, do not offer to talk to the abuser about your friend, or let yourself be seen by the abuser as a threat to their relationship.

- For copies of the leaflet on which this article was based, please write or fax: Home Office, Marketing and Communications Group, Room 157, 50 Queen Anne's Gate, London, SW1H 9AT. Fax: 020 7 273 2568

Published by the Home Office in collaboration with the Crown Prosecution Service, the Department of the Environment, Transport and the Regions, the Department of Health, the Lord Chancellor's Department, the Department of Social Security, the Welsh Office and the Women's Unit. Some material has been adapted with permission from publications of the Women's Aid Federation of England.

- The above information is from the Home Office's web site which can be found at www.homeoffice.gov.uk

© Crown copyright

Children and young people

It's not just adults who are affected by domestic abuse. Children and young people can experience the abuse of their mothers, and can also be abused themselves

What is domestic abuse?

This is when someone is being hurt or frightened by someone close to them. Usually it's a woman being hurt by her husband or boyfriend. Sometimes it can be a man being hurt by his wife or girlfriend. It also happens to gay people.

As it mostly happens to women, we will speak about your mum from now on. But everything we say could also be about your dad.

If someone is being abused they can be:

- Hit
- Shouted at
- Made a fool of
- Told they're stupid, ugly, useless
- Forced to have sex
- Kept short of money
- Locked in the house

A person who is being abused can feel:

- Sad
- Insecure
- Frightened
- Useless
- Trapped
- Angry

Is your mum being abused?

If anyone is doing any of these things to your mum, she is being abused. She may not realise that. It is common to think it is all your fault if someone is abusing you.

The only person to blame is the abuser. It is not your or your mum's fault. There is never a reason or excuse for abusing someone.

You may see your mum being hit, hear her being shouted at, or see her bruised or upset. You may have tried to stop it, to protect her. **It's important to keep yourself as safe as you can**. Your mum wouldn't want you to be hurt, too. Sometimes it's better to phone the police, or go to a neighbour for help than to try to stop it yourself.

If you think your mum is being abused, then you are also being affected. You may be feeling:

- Scared for her
- Scared for you and your brothers/sisters
- Worried about what will happen
- Worried about having to change schools
- Angry with whoever is abusing her
- Angry with yourself for not being able to stop it
- Angry with your mum for not leaving
- Or angry with her for making you leave home too.

You may be forced to join in hurting your mum as part of the abuse. **This is not your fault. It may be dangerous for you to refuse**. You could try to find a safe time to tell your mum you didn't mean it.

Are you being abused too?

When someone in a family is being abused, often other people are as well. The person who is hurting your mum may also be hurting you or your sisters/brothers. They may threaten that terrible things will happen if you tell anyone. Try to tell someone you trust – maybe another family member, trusted adult, teacher or your children's support worker if you have one.

You have done nothing wrong.

It is not your fault. Nobody should be hurting you.

Or you can contact ChildLine by phoning them free on 0800 1111. They are there 24 hours a day, every day of the year.

What if we have to leave home?

Your mum may decide that she, you and your brothers/sisters have to leave home to be safe. There are a number of places she can go for help.

She may go to the Housing Department, who will find a place for you to stay. It might be a flat in a block, with a warden to keep it safe. It might be a room in a bed and breakfast. Or it might be a house or flat you can stay in for a while.

After a while, you could be given a new house, in an area where your mum feels you would all be safe.

Another safe place to go is a refuge. They are run by an organisation called Women's Aid, which was set up to help women and children living with domestic abuse.

Refuges are usually houses which you share with other women and their children. You and your mum and sisters/brothers would have your own room and share the rest of the house. In some refuges, you would

have your own bedsit or even your own flat.

Women's Aid workers help your mum decide what to do next. Many refuges also have children's workers who can listen to you speak about what you've been through and give you support.

The refuge is a safe place, and your mum will get a break from the abuse. You will, too.

When you get rehoused from the refuge, Women's Aid workers might still keep in touch to help you get used to your new life.

What if my dad wants to see me?

Your dad might want to keep in contact with you after you've left home with your mum. He can go to court and ask for this, if she doesn't agree. If he does, you may be asked what you think by the court. This is your chance to say whatever you feel, but the court will decide what they think is best for you.

Domestic abuse affects you, too

You have a right to support for yourself. You have a right to a safe life.

What if my mum wants to go back home?

It can be very difficult to break free from someone who is abusing you. Your mum may feel she should go back to give him another chance. She may think this is the best thing for you.

If you think going home would put you at risk of abuse yourself – tell someone you trust. It may be difficult to say this to your mum. You could tell a Women's Aid worker, another relative, a teacher.

You should not be put in danger – so tell someone if you are frightened.

Child Protection Review

This is a web site which gives you the chance to find out about child protection in Scotland. Contact the Child Protection Review (www.scotland.gov.uk/childprotection) to find out more.

Domestic abuse tears lives apart

Women, children, young people, men – all across Scotland, people's lives are affected by domestic abuse.

As many as 1 in 5 women in Scotland will experience domestic abuse in their lifetime.

• The Domestic Abuse Helpline, lines open 10am-10pm. Call 0800 027 1234.

© Scottish Executive

Medics bid to end cycle of violence in abused children

Doctors have developed a dramatic new technique to prevent abused children from becoming parents who attack, and sometimes kill, their own children.

More than a third of those who are systematically beaten, injured or bullied as children go on to inflict serious harm on their own offspring. As the number of children being placed on protection registers soars, the need to break the cycle is increasingly urgent.

At an international conference on domestic violence to be held in London, at the Royal Society of Medicine, next week, Professor David Wolfe, of the University of Western Ontario, will reveal details of a revolutionary scheme, introduced in Canada, which has produced a threefold drop in this violence.

The technique involves teaching problem children how to relate to future partners. Participants – aged between 14 and 16 – are given instruction on seeking social and

By Robin McKie, Science Editor

medical help, are made to play out aggressive roles in public and assist in social work projects.

'The problem often looks inexorable,' said Wolfe. 'A child is threatened with being abandoned, gets severe beatings from a parent and is bullied by the family throughout childhood. They inflict the same thing on their own offspring.'

In Britain, a case of domestic violence is reported every six

More than a third of those who are systematically beaten, injured or bullied as children go on to inflict serious harm on their own offspring

minutes, many involving assaults on children. Last year, 29-year-old Darren Jenkinson was jailed for life in Glasgow for smothering his two baby sons. Jenkinson, who lived in 32 different children's homes before he was 16, blamed the murders on abuse he suffered at the hands of his own father.

The crucial point, says Wolfe, is to intervene before abused children become parents. The technique has proved startlingly effective. A total of 158 adolescents, each the victim of physical abuse, bullying or injury during childhood, took part in the project. Half were given treatment, the others got no help. Wolfe then followed each participant for several years.

'Those who had been helped had far better records of violence against their partners. There was a threefold reduction,' he said.

• The above article appeared in the *Observer*, 24 February 2002

© Guardian Newspapers Limited 2002

Domestic violence hurts kids too . . .

Information from Northern Ireland Women's Aid

Children, young people and domestic violence

Domestic violence is the physical, emotional, sexual or financial abuse of one person by another, with whom they have or have had an intimate relationship. Over 90% of reported cases of such violence are by men against women.

Countless children and young people in Northern Ireland are witness to domestic violence each year. These children grow up in a 'climate of fear'. In most cases they will be in the same or the next room when the violence occurs.

Although research currently exists which clearly outlines the extent of domestic violence against women and the effects on their lives, relatively little is known about the impact of violence in the home on children. As with women who live with domestic violence, every child's experiences will be different.

During violent assaults, for many children an immediate and natural reaction will be to intervene and to protect either their mother or other siblings . This may present an increased risk of physical injury to the child.

The mother/child relationship can also be affected through domestic violence.

It is important to remember that the blame for any negative impact on the mother/child relationship lies solely with the perpetrator of violence.

The impact that continual physical attacks, verbal degradation, emotional torture and social isolation can have upon a woman's life should never be underestimated or minimised.

The most important point for professionals working with families to bear in mind is that for women to provide effective protection for their children, they themselves need to be protected and supported.

Statistics				
Year	Helpline calls	Calls to advice centres and Helpline	No. of women accommodated in refuge	No. of children accommodated in refuge
1989/90		2,654	456	804
1990/91		3,735	658	982
1991/92		2,587	589	1,034
1992/93		3,238	627	1,131
1993/94		6,595	671	1,139
1994/95		8,029	737	1,234
1995/96	3,678	10,210	916	1,460
1996/97	4,235	13,484	823	1,467
1997/98	5,326	13,836	908	1,408
1998/99	8,006	17,832	1,154	1,831
1999/00	10,200	25,547	1,193	1,619
2000/01	13,600	34,796	1,076	1,465
Totals	45,045	142,543	9,908	15,574
Total women and children			**25,482**	

Source: Northern Ireland Women's Aid Federation

Effects of domestic violence on children

Domestic violence can have adverse effects on a child. It is important to remember that every child's experience of conflict will be different and every child will utilise different coping mechanisms to deal with the situation.

Some children may fail to show any negative signs at all, in fact, some may even show positive signs such as a sudden improvement in school-work. However, we should never make any assumptions about how children have been affected by domestic violence.

No symptom or syndrome inevitably follows domestic violence. There are no set patterns of how a child who has experienced violence in the home will behave.

Possible effects on children who witness domestic violence may include:
- Feelings of fear, anger, depression, grief, shame and distrust.
- A sense of powerlessness.
- Physical reactions such as stomach cramps, headaches, sleeping and eating difficulties, frequent illness.
- Slowed developmental capa-

cities, such as poor school performance, low self-esteem, difficulty relating to peers or alternatively overachieving in school.
- Behavioural problems such as running away from home, aggressive language and behaviour, becoming passive and withdrawn.
- Learning that violence is a legitimate means for resolving conflict, or for obtaining control of a situation or alternatively rejecting violence in the future and a desire to make a difference.
- Attention seeking
- Protective (of either parent).
- Resentful (towards either parent).

Ways you can help a child who has witnessed domestic violence include:
- Explain things in language that children can understand.
- Tell them that the violence is not their fault.
- Give them permission to talk about the violence.
- Help make a safety plan which they can follow.
- Find them someone outside the family with whom they can share their feelings.

- Let them know that others have had similar experiences.
- Ring and discuss the situation with Women's Aid and/or Social Services to find out how else you can help the children.

Information for mothers

'He hits me, but he's good to the kids.'

This is commonly said by women subjected to domestic violence. A father showing attention or affection to his children cannot make up for denying them (through his violence towards their mother) their right to a safe and happy childhood and family environment.

There is still a prevailing attitude in society that mothers should be 'perfect' and almost wholly responsible for their children's well-being. This attitude can lead to blaming the mother even when the father is perpetrating the violence. You may be feeling responsible for your partner's violence, and for the impact his behaviour is having on the children. Remember you are not to blame for his violence, and you are not responsible for the effect his abuse towards you has had on your children.

You need help, so you can help your children

No matter how caring a parent you are, at some level your ability to do your best for your children will be affected by your partner's violence. Sadly, this is a time then your children are likely to need your care and attention more than ever.

Difficult choices

Concern for your children is probably a major factor (if not the major factor) in whether you decide to separate from an abusive partner. It is likely to be confusing and difficult for you to weigh up which situation is best for your children.

You may have thought:
- He says he will get custody of the kids.
- How can I take them away from their dad whom they love, their home, their pets, their school?
- Can I offer the children anything better?
- Are we in more danger if we leave?

The following suggestions may assist you in caring for your children, and in making choices about your situation.

If you are living with an abusive partner:
- To enable you to help your children you need to get help too.
- Even though your children may not have been in the room, they will have been able to sense the atmosphere, so if you can, explain to them what is happening.
- Let them know it is not their role to protect you.
- Let them know that you want to know how they feel.
- Assure them that feeling frightened, angry, confused or sad is normal in the situation.
- Find a trustworthy, empathetic adult that the kids can talk to (i.e. school counsellor, relative).

If you have separated, or are leaving the situation you can:
- Seek advice and support for yourself and your children.
- Encourage your children to talk about how they are feeling.
- Take favourite toys and some of your children's other items.
- Seek parenting support.
- Contact Women's Aid.
- Tell your children of your plans for the future.
- Seek legal aid.

Women's Aid response to young people

The majority of women who come to refuges have children. Children arriving at the refuge may react in a variety of ways to the change of circumstance as well as to the history of violence. Through time, all children reach a better understanding of their situation by being sensitively helped to identify and deal with their feelings.

A refuge is a safe house where you can live free from violence. It offers temporary accommodation and a breathing space where decisions can be made free from pressure and fear.

A wide range of play activities and materials are used by workers as an integral part of life in the refuge.

Child workers in refuges will be sensitive to the needs of individual children and will look for opportunities to help those with difficulties. Children need explanations about what is happening and why, plus lots of reassurance of love and care. They do have coping strategies of their own and these can be developed by understanding them. During play children can relax. Children are not confined to the refuge as there are sometimes outside activities such as swimming, visits to the museum, zoo, disco, skating, park and beach.

Taking part in social activities restores normality to children and mothers are encouraged to get their children back to school as soon as possible.

The easier it becomes for children to talk about problems the more supported and accepted they will feel.

Women's Aid also provides support for women and their children who have not stayed in a refuge. This is provided through aftercare and outreach projects and in the advice centres.

One crucial element in the recovery process is provision of support. Support may take many forms and may be offered by various individuals and agencies working with women and children on a regular basis. Organisations and individuals coming into contact with families need to be aware of signs and symptoms of domestic violence. Policies and procedures need to be developed and put in place to ensure that women and children are receiving the support and information they need either to stay and survive in the situation or to leave.

Children need supportive adults who will listen to them and help them come to terms with their own situations. For adults to be supportive they need to understand how children are affected and develop positive responses in working with them.

• The above information is an extract from a leaflet by Northern Ireland Women's Aid. See page 41 for their address details.

© *Northern Ireland Women's Aid*

Women's Aid is for children and young people too!

Who are Women's Aid?

Women's Aid works with women, children and young people under the age of 16 years, who come from all different backgrounds. This does not mean that we do not support young people over 16. If a young person over 16 does not want to or cannot use our service we will support them and their family to find other agencies that can help, sometimes finding them somewhere else that they can stay and feel safe.

Sometimes women just want to talk to someone about what is happening in their home and we may never meet the children and young people who live there. Other times we will meet children and young people at our office or in their home. There are times however that women decide it is safer for everyone to move into one of our refuges. This might be for a short time to give everyone some breathing space before they go back home or they might decide to stay until they get a new house or until the person who is abusing them leaves their home.

What is a refuge?

The refuge is a safe place for women, children and young people under 16 years who have lived with abuse. You may live with other families, but your family will have a room of your own. Everyone will be trying to get away from being hurt for a while. There might be children and young people of all ages, so it can sometimes feel quite busy, but you can also make new friends as well. The refuges can be very different from each other. They can be a single house on their own, they can be in a tenement, some refuges have resources for women, children and young people who experience disability or who are from a black or ethnic minority background. Sometimes refuges have workers that are there specifically for children and young people. This does not mean

that they do not talk to the women, but the children and young people are their priority. If there is not a children/young person's worker you can talk to other workers. It is important to us that you feel you can talk to someone. We know how hard it can be. Whatever is worrying you, we will try to support you while you settle in. This might mean supporting you if you have to change schools, letting you know about the local area or just giving you space to talk. At first it might be hard but hopefully it will get better. There will be workers to help and listen if you want. You have the right to feel safe and to be listened to.

Hope for the future

We hope this has given you a better idea about what Women's Aid is all about and that if you are in touch with us now or in the future you will feel more comfortable when you talk to us. There are other people that can support you however and we have put their names and telephone numbers below. These numbers are free and will not show up on the telephone bill unless you are using a mobile phone.

ChildLine
0800 1111
Helpline for children and young people on any issue

Scottish Child Law Centre
0800 317500
Helpline for under-18s

Get Connected
0800 096 0096
Helpline which will put you in touch with services that can help you.

• The above information is from the Scottish Women's Aid's web site which can be found at www.scottishwomensaid.co.uk Alternatively, see page 41 for their address details.

© Scottish Women's Aid

Domestic violence

Are you a victim?

By Jill Curtis

Violence in the home is a crime we are all becoming more aware of each year. In the UK a quarter of all reported violent crimes are domestic. In the US the estimate of the number ranges from 960,000 incidents of violence against a current or former partner to four million each year. But domestic violence is also a world-wide problem.

What is violence – or abuse? It is about power, and this can be about controlling a partner by either physical or emotional abuse. It is rarely a one-off event. There are also many different forms of abuse, and physical attack is only one of them. Perhaps most of us think of a black eye or broken arm, but sex can be used as a way of dominating a partner. So can ridicule. So can control of family finance. So, too, can shouting and screaming.

Does your partner accuse you of all manner of 'crimes'? These may even be everyday events, such as looking out of the car window to look at other men or talking for too long to friends and family on the telephone! Jealousy is a formidable spur for many attacks.

Do you feel under threat of violence? Have you been on the receiving end of a violent attack? Do you have to 'account' for time spent away from home? Does emotional or verbal abuse play a part in your relationship?

Psychological abuse can at times be even more damaging than physical abuse. It can be something which whittles away at your self-esteem until you may even begin to *believe* that you are 'stupid', 'useless' or that you 'deserve it'. Attempts at retaliating may bring further violence: tears of frustration and helplessness are ridiculed and mocked. If this is happening to you it may make it even more difficult to break away and do something about your situation. Loss of self-esteem, and being made to believe you are 'worthless' make it difficult to think about getting help. Does this sound familiar? You may also be on the receiving end of blackmail, for that is what it is, if your partner threatens to kill himself – or herself – if you leave. Or to harm the children.

Sometimes there is a warning that violence is imminent, and this may be triggered by alcohol or drug abuse. Other times an attack can come out of the blue.

Violence against women is only part of the problem. It is sometimes the woman who is violent towards her man. This is known as the hidden side of domestic violence. For a man to be on the receiving end of abuse is often seen as a comic situation, and sadly this adds to the reluctance men have to come forward and speak about it. But it happens all the same. The humiliation which accompanies this abuse makes it just as hard for men to break free and seek help. Erin Pizzey, who founded the first refuge for battered women and children in London, England, now speaks of her concerns for men as well.

On the Internet there are several different support groups for women on the receiving end of violence. And in the US, Australia and New Zealand I could find help for men, but it was virtually impossible to find help for men in the UK. I wonder why this should be so?

One survey in the US discovered that where women have been

> *Sometimes there is a warning that violence is imminent, and this may be triggered by alcohol or drug abuse. Other times an attack can come out of the blue*

accused of violence towards men it was not as one might suppose from self-defence, but as a reaction to men not paying attention or listening to them. I am not the judge, but these must have been very desperate women. Not that resorting to violence can ever be the right thing to do.

The Department of Justice reports that every 37.8 seconds somewhere a man is battered in the US. Every 20.9 seconds a woman is battered. Frightening figures. The Home Office in the UK reported in their survey into domestic violence that women are more likely to be badly injured and to suffer repeated attacks than men. But domestic violence is a two-way street not to be tolerated whichever way it goes. No one should live their day-to-day life in fear of another.

The question often asked is, why do people stay in an abusive relationship? The most common reason is because of financial restraints or fear of losing the children. It is easy from the outside to say 'get out' but often there is hope that 'things will get better' or shame at saying to an outsider 'I am being beaten'. There is sometimes a mistaken belief that love will conquer all. This usually covers up a reluctance to bring things to a head and face all the changes that a challenge might bring about.

If there are children in a relationship this brings with it added worries. All research shows that if children witness their parents' marital discord and fighting, this will affect them deeply and their emotional well-being will be harmed. They will be scared by what they see and hear. Don't trick yourself into believing that they do not notice, or will not be affected by it.

The sites I found most helpful on the Internet were where addresses or telephone numbers of refuges were listed and where it was indicated that although in the main these were for women and children, they were also sympathetic towards men who needed help. There is help 'out there' so don't be afraid of looking for it. There are people who will listen, and help you to decide upon the best course. They will also provide some guidelines to assist you with your own safety, and that of your children. Be on guard, too, even if you have left your abusive partner, since you need to keep alert.

If any or all of this rings a bell with you, or you know of someone who is being abused, don't hesitate, get help and protection now. Some men and women have delayed, and tragically they are no longer alive.

• The above information is an extract from www.familyonwards.com. Jill Curtis is a senior psychotherapist working in the UK. Over the past three years Jill Curtis has developed

the web site, which has over a hundred articles on it and a continually expanding section of reviews of books on family issues. She has also contributed to a variety of other web sites connected with

parenting, families, self-help, divorce, gay issues and women's interests. Her web site and articles constantly receive enthusiastic praise.

© Jill Curtis 2002

Refuge

A national lifeline for women and children experiencing domestic violence

Refuge is the UK's largest single provider of specialist accommodation and support to women and children escaping domestic violence. Refuge has grown from a small charity operating the world's first women's refuge in Chiswick in 1971, to a national lifeline for up to 80,000 women and children every year.

At Refuge, we recognise that reaching a place of safety is only the first step in rebuilding a future free from abuse. Uniquely, through our holistic and integrated services providing practical and emotional support, we empower women and help children towards brighter futures free from violence.

Domestic violence – the facts

'Domestic violence represents 25 per cent of all recorded violent crime in Britain, yet it is a crime which our society often prefers to ignore . . . Refuge is a lifeline.'

Cherie Booth QC,
Refuge Trustee

• Over their lifetime, 23% of women report being a victim of domestic assault,[1] and in 35% of

households where assault has occurred, a second incident takes place within five weeks of the first.[2]
• One woman in nine is severely beaten by her partner every year.[3]
• In 1997, 55,000 UK women moved into refuge accommodation to escape domestic violence.
• 38% of women calling Refuge's national 24-hour domestic violence helpline are at the point of separation and in urgent need of support and emergency accommodation.
• 85% of callers have children (three on average) who they fear are also in danger.
• Department of the Environment figures for 1997 show that 19% of homeless households had been made homeless due to domestic violence – some 19,320 households in total.
• Sine 1981, the largest increase in violent crimes has been incidents of domestic violence, yet domestic violence is the least likely violent crime to be reported to the police. Only one in three crimes resulting in injury are reported.[4]

• 1998 Homicide Statistics showed that, every week, two women in England and Wales are killed by their partner or ex-partner. 1997 statistics showed that 47% of female homicide victims were killed by a current or former partner, compared to 8% of men.

References

1 Home Office. *British Crime Survey 1999.*
2 Home Office Briefing Note, *Assessing and managing the risk of Domestic Violence*, Sylvia Walby and Andrew Myhill, University of Leeds, Jan 2000.
3 Elizabeth Stanko et al. *Counting the Costs: Estimating the Impact of Domestic Violence in the London Borough of Hackney* Swindon: Crime Concern, 1997.
4 Home Office. *British Crime Survey 1996.*

• Sandra Horley's book, *Power and Control: Why charming men can make dangerous lovers*, is published by Vermillion £7.99 and available in all good bookshops. See page 41 for Refuge's address details.

© Refuge

Refuges

Information from the Scottish Executive

What is a refuge?

Refuge is a safe place for you to stay if you need to leave home because of abuse.

You can stay as long as you need. You can take your children with you, if you have any.

You can go back as many times as you need to.

You and your children can get support to help you recover from your experiences and plan a new life, if that's what you want.

Who runs refuges?

Refuges are run by Women's Aid groups, all over Scotland. Or you can find information about your local group in the phone book, or from the police, housing department or social work department.

How do I get into a refuge?

You can contact Women's Aid through the office phone numbers listed, or visit during their advertised opening hours.

Or you can phone the Domestic Abuse Helpline on 0800 027 1234 between 10am and 10pm, any day of the week. The Helpline can put you in touch with your local group, or a group in another area if you would not feel safe locally.

Who can go?

Any woman who has experienced domestic abuse. You don't have to have been beaten up, or have bruises.

You don't have to prove what has happened to you. Women's Aid will believe what you say and try to give you the help you need.

Some refuges have facilities for disabled women and children and there are two groups providing services for black and minority ethnic women and children.

You can take your children with you, if you have any. However, boys over 16 years of age are not usually allowed to stay in the refuge. If this applies to you, you would be given help to find an alternative, safe place for your son/s to stay.

How long for?

As long as it takes to achieve whatever option you have chosen. This could be just one night, or a weekend, if you just want a breathing space. It could be a week or two while you think things through and find out what choices you have. It could be a few months or even longer while you wait to be rehoused.

You will be supported to decide what you want to do and given all the information you need to make that choice.

You may go back home and decide you want to return if things don't work out. That's OK, there is no limit to the number of times you can stay in refuge.

What are they like?

It varies – some are ordinary council houses, some are buildings that have been adapted, and some are purpose built.

You might have one room which you will share with your children, while the rest of the house is shared with other families. Or you may have a bedsit, or a flat within a larger block. Many refuges have facilities for children, where they can receive support and take part in activities which help them understand what they have been through.

There are refuges all over Scotland – in towns and cities, in rural and island areas. If you wouldn't be safe in your own area, you can go to any refuge in Britain which has a space. Refuges usually have a few simple rules which they ask everyone to keep – no pets, male visitors and illegal drugs. Some refuges have other rules about alcohol. Women's Aid workers will explain all this to you.

It's not your own home, and it can be a bit chaotic at times. It can be stressful living with other people and coping with different standards of cleaning and child care and so on. But refuges can really change lives – you can take things at your own pace, you will find your confidence growing as time passes and you will see that you can have a different life.

Confidentiality

Confidentiality is very important – the refuge addresses and telephone

numbers are not made public, for everyone's safety. You must be very careful who you give this information to – even if you trust them, they might be put in a difficult position if your abuser thinks they will know how to contact you.

If you have a mobile phone, you might think about keeping it switched off, so that you can't be contacted.

Refuge staff

Refuge staff are all women, and have been trained to support you and your children during your stay.

They understand what you have been through and can help you make decisions about how to move forward.

They have the information you will need, and can also refer you to others for specialist help.

They will not blame you for what has happened, or try to make you do what they think you should do. It's your life, and you have to be the one to make the decisions. Refuge workers will support you whatever you decide.

If you decide to go back home to try again, they will understand why, although they may be worried about your safety.

Children

Children often enjoy living in refuge, because there is a lot going on and different people about. Many refuges have children's workers, who support the children, help them to under-stand what has been happening at home and explain that it wasn't their, or your, fault. They also arrange outings and activities, so there's something to keep them occupied.

Children of all ages stay in refuge, from tiny babies to young people. Older children can find refuge more difficult – if they have to share a room with mum and younger brothers and sisters for example. More and more refuges will have self-contained accommodation soon, and some already do.

It can be hard for children to understand why they had to leave home, dad, their toys, friends, pets and maybe school. Refuge and children's workers can help you explain and work with the children so that they see why abuse is not acceptable.

Profile

Maggie is 35 years old. She has been married to John for 14 years, and has two children – Mark aged 12 and Katie aged 9. John has a good job in the education field and Maggie has not been allowed to work since they got married. They have a large house in a nearby town and a good standard of living.

John has been violent to Maggie since their marriage. He regularly assaulted her, often causing injuries. He is also extremely possessive, constantly accuses her of having affairs and controls what she wears, how she does her hair, what make-up she wears. John has threatened Maggie that he will kill the children and then her if she tries to leave. He has also threatened to kill himself, and has attempted to do so.

Maggie went to her local Women's Aid group when she had reached the stage of believing that she had to get out before she was killed. She and the children moved into refuge, and the children started going to the local school. John used his contacts to track the children to their new school.

Maggie found refuge life difficult at first, as she wasn't used to sharing. The children were unhappy at having to move schools and were unsettled and frightened when their father turned up at the school gates.

Maggie thought about going home, about moving to another refuge, about taking the children and just disappearing. But she had begun to enjoy life in the refuge, getting support from the other women, sitting up till all hours at night sharing experiences.

John continued to make life as difficult as he could for Maggie, but she now felt stronger, and decided to stay where she was rather than letting John force her into moving again. The children enjoyed the activities organised by the children's worker and liked having other children around to play with. John hadn't allowed them much contact with other children at home.

After a long stay of nearly a year, Maggie was rehoused, quite close to the refuge. She worked hard to get the house in shape, and enjoyed the challenge of furnishing it on a low budget. One favourite find was an ancient and enormous American fridge, which took up most of the kitchen.

Once she had moved in, Maggie held a party for the women she had shared the refuge with and the Women's Aid workers who had supported her during her stay. She kept in contact for a while, asking for a reference when she applied for a college course.

Eventually, the family home was sold, and Maggie bought a small flat with her share of the proceeds. The children are settled and happy, and Maggie is working, something she was never allowed to do while she was with John. It wasn't always easy, but Maggie says refuge changed her life.

It's fairly common for children to 'act up' when they come to refuge. They are just testing out the boundaries in this new situation, and most soon calm down. Everyone understands, and won't blame you or think you are a bad mother.

It can be hard for children to understand why they had to leave home, dad, their toys, friends, pets and maybe school

---

What next?

Refuge is temporary accommodation, and so you will be supported to decide what you want to do next. There are a number of options, and you will be given all the information you need to help you make your mind up.

If you decide to go home and try again, you may be able to keep in touch with Women's Aid, if you can do it safely. If you decide to take legal action of some sort, you will be put in touch with a sympathetic solicitor and supported until that is resolved.

If you decide to apply for rehousing, you will be helped throughout that process. You can stay in the refuge as long as it takes.

You will be helped to furnish and equip your new house, and supported when you move in if you want.

Many friendships start in refuge, and other women are often your best source of support. Whatever you decide to do, remember you are not alone. There are people who understand, and can help.

Will I be able to cope on my own?

Moving on in your life can be exciting, but it can also be frightening. It's very common to be anxious about whether or not you'll be able to cope on your own. You may never have lived on your own, or you may not have been allowed to have control of your own money as part of the abuse.

Perhaps you're worried about the children – will they run riot without another adult to discipline them? Or doing things around the house – what if you need to change a fuse and you've never done it before?

First of all – remember what you've coped with by living with domestic abuse. That's not easy, but you did it. And you left and stayed away, which isn't easy either.

There are people who can help in all sorts of ways – you can learn to budget or manage on a small income, do maintenance or decorating around the house, find out how best to deal with the children.

Women's Aid workers can help, or can put you in touch with others who can help you feel more confident about coping.

Ask for help – don't worry by yourself.

• The Domestic Abuse Helpline, lines open 10am-10pm Call 0800 027 1234.

© Scottish Executive

Safe as houses

Paul Humphries on a scheme to stop domestic violence by getting guilty men out of the family home and into counselling

Today, in Sunderland, at least 13 women will be attacked and beaten by their male partners. The number may be even higher than that. Police can only record the incidents they are called to, and social workers believe the true figure may be more like 40.

Like other female victims of domestic violence across Britain, the women of Wearside have, until now, been given little option when they want to escape a violent partner. If they crave a halt to the beatings and the abuse, they have to flee the family home and seek refuge with other battered women and their children.

But, in Sunderland, a scheme is being developed where, instead of battered women being forced into refuges, it will be the perpetrators of the violence who are removed from the family home. They will be placed in a specially staffed hostel, where they will undergo counselling. The scheme hinges partly on a tenancy agreement drawn up by Sunderland Housing Group, which has taken over the running of the city council's 36,000 properties. Under the agreement, any tenant responsible for domestic violence is deemed to have broken the contract and must leave the property.

Sharon Kane, coordinator of the Wearside Domestic Violence Forum, says: 'Why should the woman, who is the innocent party, be the one to have to leave the family home? Instead, we are going to provide accommodation for the perpetrators of domestic violence and offer them help if they are prepared to change.'

The statistics for Sunderland and surrounding districts make shocking reading. Eight hundred women and children, all fleeing violent men, were turned away in 2000 from local refuges – one in the city itself and another in nearby Washington. Each has only 30 beds, providing space for an average of just 11 families.

Last November alone, police in Sunderland's three operational districts were called out to 390 incidents of domestic violence. 'In our experience, you can probably treble that figure,' says Kane. 'Then look at what percentage of these

---

'Why should the woman, who is the innocent party, be the one to have to leave the family home?'

---

attacks are in the high-risk category – that could be 20% – and you have a better picture of what is really happening.'

A clause in a tenancy agreement making domestic violence a case for eviction is not a new initiative, either in Sunderland or elsewhere, but linking it to a specific programme of counselling for violent men who want to change, and who will not be allowed back into the house until they do, is a radical departure.

The Sunderland Housing Group works closely with the domestic violence forum and is helping find a property in which to set up the hostel. John Craggs, speaking for the group, says the clause has been in the tenancy agreement 'for quite some time', but he cannot remember any man being evicted for domestic violence.

'We have been taking domestic violence seriously as a housing issue for a very long time,' Craggs says. 'The provision has existed and there has been intent to support, but it has never been taken up. It has been the situation normally that the woman has wanted to leave the house, and then wouldn't return.'

But that will now change once the hostel is up and running, believes Clare Phillipson, one of the workers at Wearside Women In Need and, by general agreement, the driving force behind the scheme. 'What we have had is women who are the victims of domestic violence saying their male partner will have nowhere to go if they throw them out, or they fear that the man will kill himself if he is evicted,' she says.

'But they will soon not have those concerns. We will be offering somewhere for the men to go and live; to receive counselling and learn how to address their behaviour; to realise they have committed a serious crime and that they have to change.'

Phillipson is adamant that battered women must not see their only options as staying at home and living in fear of attack, or fleeing to a refuge. She welcomes the chance to work with the city's biggest landlord in seeing that women get a better deal. She quotes an instance where one social landlord in the north-east threatened to evict a woman if the sound of her male partner beating her up got any worse. The neighbours were complaining.

'That's why it's good to work with Sunderland Housing,' says Phillipson. 'We all know that we're pulling in the same direction.'

The scheme will cost some £200,000 to set up, then £150,000 a year to run. But the groups involved are confident they will be able to raise the money needed through various funding agencies. 'It is incredibly cost-effective,' says Phillipson. 'What is the cost of the damage done by violent men to women and children? That's a figure that can't be calculated.'

• Wearside Women in Need is on 0191-416 3550.

© Guardian Newspapers Limited 2002

Men learning to end their violence to women

Information from CHANGE

CHANGE was established in 1989 to meet a recognised need for a means to challenge and change men who are violent to women. When the phenomenon of domestic violence was 'discovered' in the 1970s, the emphasis, quite rightly, by activists and campaigners was on gaining recognition of the existence and extent of the problem, and the need for services to protect women and children. This was not an easy task. For nearly thirty years Women's Aid has been the organisation in Britain which has been in the forefront of this work. They have offered practical help and emotional support to countless women and their children who have suffered violence and abuse in its many forms, as well as challenging institutional and community tolerance of men's violence and campaigning for social change and legal reforms.

Until fairly recently the focus has left the perpetrators, although condemned for their violence in principle, chiefly untouched. A growing body of evidence has revealed that domestic violence is widespread and overwhelmingly perpetrated on women by men. However these men remained invisible and largely unaccountable

for their behaviour. In the late 1980s, spurred on by government plans to divert offenders away from prosecution, some activists in Scotland were considering how domestic violence offenders could better be dealt with by the courts. It was acknowledged that the usual fines and probation orders were unsatisfactory in holding offenders to account or promoting women's safety. Growing awareness of work in America, in particular of the Domestic Abuse Intervention Project in Duluth, Minnesota, led to plans to pilot re-education programmes for abusive men which required them to take responsibility for their abuse and learn other ways of relating to their partner.

CHANGE was the first project in Europe to set up a programme of re-education for violent men which aims to take full account of the interests of women and children. CHANGE began as a pilot project

in September 1989 with the central aim of providing a criminal-justice-based re-education programme for men convicted of offences involving violence towards their wives or female partners.

In order to highlight the criminal and unacceptable nature of men's violence to women the programme operated as a sanction of the justice system. By locating the work within the justice system it demonstrates to men, to women and to the community at large that violence to any member of that community is illegal and socially unacceptable. Issues about the safety of women and children involved were taken into account and CHANGE shared with Women's Aid a feminist analysis of the roots of men's violence. That analysis sees men's violence to partners as intentional, albeit not always conscious, and as but one aspect of a whole range of abusive behaviours, which have the purpose of maintaining male dominance over women. That male dominance is rooted in history and culture and reflected in institutional responses and traditional community tolerance of marital violence.

Aims

CHANGE started its work in 1989 with three clear aims. First, to devise and operate a programme for men, and to work with other agencies to provide services to women. Second, to work to encourage a multi-agency response to domestic violence; and third to develop training programmes and educational materials on this topic.

The CHANGE men's programme was formally evaluated alongside the work of Edinburgh's programme, the DVPP, and an important finding for the future was that:

'a significant proportion of the offenders who participated in the men's programmes reduced their violence and associated controlling behaviour and their women partners reported significant improvements in the quality of their lives and their relationships with these men'.

Dobash, R.E., Dobash, R. P., Cavanagh, K., & Lewis, R. (1996), *Research Evaluation of Programmes for*

Typically men are anxious to explain away the violence in several ways which include numerous examples of denial, minimisation and blame

---

Violent Men, The Scottish Office Central Research Unit, Edinburgh

Training other agencies to implement this work now forms the main task of the organisation. CHANGE is currently funded by the Scottish Executive to undertake a National Training Initiative to promote effective practice. This is targeted at local authority criminal-justice staff and relevant partner agencies.

Understanding the problem

In CHANGE's experience, men who use violence and abuse to partners do so because they believe at some level that they are entitled to. Specifically violence/abuse is used to enforce obedience or compliance in the form of recognition of authority (e.g. punishing her for 'answering back') and provision of services (meeting his needs: e.g., his tea on the table) or just to 'show who's boss'. Sexual jealousy is often present or apparent.

Typically men are anxious to explain away the violence in several

ways which include numerous examples of denial, minimisation and blame. They describe the violence as a one-off event, as something which they cannot recall because it happened so quickly, or because they were drunk or under the influence of drugs, or because they were so enraged that they 'saw red' at the time. They will employ a whole spectrum of excuses and pressures in order to excuse or justify their actions.

The use of denial, minimisation and blame is typical of human behaviour when feelings of guilt, shame or fear of reprisals exist. They are of course techniques of neutralisation employed universally to make individuals feel better or more justified in behaving in a certain way. Abusive men typically blame partners for provoking the violence/abuse, minimise its seriousness and deny responsibility. Common expressions include:

- 'She winds me up!'
- 'She asked for it!'
- 'The house was a mess!'
- 'Her kids were acting up!'
- 'She wouldn't shut up!'
- 'She bruises easily!'
- 'I was drunk!'
- 'I can't remember what I did!'

Men behave in a variety of ways when forced to confront the fact that they have used violence to a partner.

• The above information is from CHANGE's web site which can be found at www.changeweb.org.uk
© CHANGE

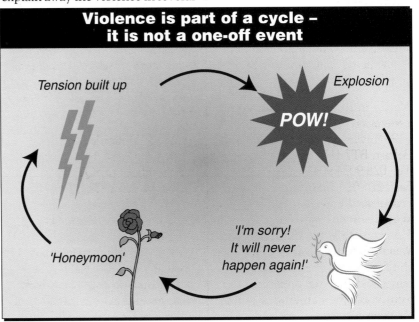

Violence is part of a cycle – it is not a one-off event

Tension built up

Explosion

POW!

'I'm sorry! It will never happen again!'

'Honeymoon'

ADDITIONAL RESOURCES

You might like to contact the following organisations for further information. Due to the increasing cost of postage, many organisations cannot respond to enquiries unless they receive a stamped, addressed envelope.

Barnardo's
Tanners Lane
Barkingside
Ilford, IG6 1QG
Tel: 020 8550 8822
Fax: 020 8551 6870
E-mail:
media.team@barnardos.org.uk
Web site: www.barnardos.org.uk
Barnardo's works with over 47,000 children, young people and their families in more than 300 projects across the county. This includes work with children affected by today's most urgent issues.

CHANGE
4-6 South Lumley Street
Grangemouth, FK3 8BT
Tel: 01324 485595
Fax: 01324 486344
Web site: www.changeweb.org.uk
CHANGE offers training and consultancy to Criminal Justice Service staff and partner agencies to promote effective practice in implementing and managing criminal-justice-based re-education programmes for men convicted of violence towards their wives or female partners.

Hidden Hurt
19 Parkfield Rank
Pucklechurch
Bristol, BS16 9NR
E-mail: contact@hiddenhurt.co.uk
Web site: www.hiddenhurt.co.uk
A UK-based Abuse Information and Support Site.

Northern Ireland Women's Aid Federation
129 University Street
Belfast, BT7 1HP
Tel: 028 9024 9041
Fax 028 9023 9296
E-mail: niwaf@dnet.co.uk
Web site: www.niwaf.org
The aims of the Northern Ireland Women's Aid Federation (NIWAF) are – the provision of refuge and ongoing support to women and their children suffering abuse within the home; to

encourage a process of self-help and recognition of the emotional needs of children involved in domestic violence. 24-hour help line 028 90 331818.

NSPCC – National Society for the Prevention of Cruelty to Children
National Centre, 42 Curtain Road
London, EC2A 3NH
Tel: 020 7825 2500
Fax: 020 7825 2525
E-mail: info@nspcc.org.uk
Web site: www.nspcc.org.uk
Has a network of Child Protection Teams and projects to protect children from abuse. Can help parents, carers and relatives who feel they may be in danger of harming their children.
Operates the Child Protection Helpline offering counselling and support. Tel: 0800 800 5000.

Refuge
2-8 Maltravers Street
London, WC2R 3EE
Tel: 020 7395 7700
Fax: 020 7395 7721
E-mail: info@refuge.org.uk
Refuge provides accommodation and a unique range of professional, high-quality services for over 650 abused women and children each year. Produces publications about the work of Refuge and facts about domestic violence. If you are a woman needing advice or help call the 24-hour National Domestic Violence HelpLine on 0870 599 5443.

Scottish Women's Aid
Norton Park, 57 Albion Road
Edinburgh, EH7 5QY
Tel: 0131 475 2372
Fax: 0131 475 2384
E-mail: swa2swa-l.demon.co.uk
Web site:
www.scottishwomensaid.co.uk
Scottish Women's Aid is a confidential organisation which provides information, support and safe refuge for women, children

and young people who are experiencing or have experienced domestic abuse. Produces leaflets on domestic violence, the law, parental rights and responsibilities and young people's rights.

Women Against Rape (WAR)
Crossroads Women's Centre
230a Kentish Town
London, NW5 2AB
Tel: 020 7482 2496
Fax: 020 7209 4761
Web site:
www.womenagainstrape.net
Provides support, counselling, legal advice and information for women and girls who have been raped, sexually assaulted or who have suffered other violence including domestic violence.

Women's Aid Federation of England (WAFE)
PO Box 391
Bristol, BS99 7WS
Tel: 0117 944 4411
Fax: 0117 924 1703
E-mail: info@womensaid.org.uk
Web site: www.womensaid.org.uk
Provides advice, information and temporary refuge for women and their children who are threatened by mental, emotional or physical violence, harassment, or sexual abuse. Runs the Women's Aid National Domestic Violence Helpline: 08457 023 468. Mon-Thurs 10am-5pm; Fri 10am-3pm. Produces leaflets, books and resources. Ask for their publications list.

YWCA
Clarendon House
52 Cornmarket Street
Oxford, OX1 3EJ
Tel: 01865 304200
Fax: 01865 204805
E-mail: info@ywca-gb.org.uk
Web site: www.ywca-gb.org.uk
The YWCA in England and Wales is a force for change for women who are facing discrimination and inequalities of all kinds.

INDEX

ACKNOWLEDGEMENTS

The publisher is grateful for permission to reproduce the following material.

While every care has been taken to trace and acknowledge copyright, the publisher tenders its apology for any accidental infringement or where copyright has proved untraceable. The publisher would be pleased to come to a suitable arrangement in any such case with the rightful owner.

Chapter One: Domestic Violence

Abuse in the family, © Northern Ireland Women's Aid Federation, *Domestic violence facts*, © 2001 Women's Aid Federation of England, *What is domestic abuse?*, © Scottish Women's Aid, *Incidence*, © Domestic Violence Data Source, *Prevalence and incidence*, © Domestic Violence Data Source, *Prevalence*, © Domestic Violence Data Source, *Domestic violence*, © Barnardo's, *A few home truths about domestic violence*, © Women Against Rape, *Key facts*, © Domestic Violence Data Source, *The impact of domestic violence*, © Domestic Violence Data Source, *Effect of domestic violence*, © Domestic Violence Data Source, *Study to find out true cost of domestic violence*, © Guardian Newspapers Limited 2002, *Children and domestic violence*, © Hidden Hurt, *Domestic violence gives warning of child abuse*, © NSPCC 2002, *A case study from the NSPCC*, © NSPCC 2002, *The truth about domestic violence*, © Domestic Violence Intervention Project, *Hitting home*, © YWCA, '*The thing is, I still love her*', © Guardian Newspapers Limited 2002, *Domestic violence: is the law letting women down?*, © Steve Tooze, Woman's Own, *Victims of domestic violence*, © Steve Tooze, Woman's Own.

Chapter Two: Seeking Help

Break the chain, © Crown copyright is reproduced with the permission of the Controller of Her Majesty's Stationery Office, *Children and young people*, © Scottish Executive, *Medics bid to end cycle of violence in abused children*, © Guardian Newspapers Limited 2002, *Domestic violence hurts kids too . . .*, © Northern Ireland Women's Aid Federation, *Statistics*, © Northern Ireland Women's Aid Federation, *Women's Aid is for children and young people too!*, © Scottish Women's Aid, *Domestic violence*, © Jill Curtis 2002, *Refuge*, © Refuge, *Refuges*, © Scottish Executive, *Safe as houses*, © Guardian Newspapers Limited 2002, *Men learning to end their violence to women*, © CHANGE.

Photographs and illustrations:

Pages 1, 9, 14: Fiona Katauskas; pages 3, 20, 28, 35: Bev Aisbett; pages 7, 13, 22, 26, 33, 39: Simon Kneebone; pages 25, 29, 36: Pumpkin House.

Craig Donnellan
Cambridge
September, 2002